IMAGE

FRED GREGORY

CREATESPACE

© Fred Gregory 2014
All rights reserved. This book is protected by the copyright laws of the United States of America. This book may not be copied or reprinted for Commercial gain or profit. The use of short quotations or occasional page for personal or group study is permitted and encouraged.

All scripture references are from *Authorized King James Version*

Imagination

ISBN 13: 978-1497336209
ISBN 10: 1497336201

CONTENTS

Dedication……………………………………………………7

Forward………………………………………………………9

Acknowledgements………………………………………...13

Endorsements………………………………………………...15

Chapter One
Thy Kingdom Come Thy Will Be Done……………………17

Chapter Two
Imagination Plumbed Deeper………………………………37

Chapter Three
Mysteries of the Kingdom of God…………………………..65

Chapter Four
The Transition………………………………………………81

Chapter Five
Application…………………………………………………93

Chapter Six
Comparing Spiritual to Spiritual..101

Chapter Seven
Sozo/Shabar 111

Chapter Eight
The Secret Place of the Most High......................................123

Endnotes..130

DEDICATION

I dedicate this book to my beloved wife of forty-eight years, Norma J. Gregory. I also dedicate this effort to my parents Mervin Gregory and Mary Gregory (Deceased).

FORWARD

In nineteen eighty-seven, I wrote a term paper for my English 101 class. The paper was entitled, "Thy Kingdom Come". My teacher, Mr. Walter Holden, an agnostic, said later that he almost did not let me write on this topic because he didn't think that I could find enough research material on it. He really meant resources besides the Bible. I got an A + for the work.

In the thesis paragraph of that paper, I asked the question, "If that prayer, prayed weekly all over the world "THY KINGDOM COME, THY WILL BE DONE ON EARTH AS IN HEAVEN," is answered in the affirmative, what will it mean?"

In light of the revelation that I received below, some twenty-one years later, that paper was prophetic.

THE WORD OF GOD

MAY 4TH, 2008

The word of the Lord came to Fred Gregory, just an ordinary human being, this the 4th day of May 2008.

There is a hunger in the Church for the deeper things of God. Thy Kingdom Come!
When that prayer is answered in the affirmative by **THE LORD GOD ALMIGHTY:** *Signs & Wonders like the world has never known will be demonstrated by the "laity" from children to the ancient—in their everyday living.*

No longer will God's people be honored, *just* for their *"faithfulness"* in horrible situations.

In MY KINGDOM, platitudes and endurance will be replaced by results in the spiritual and in the physical realms.

The war is raging. Enter **MY KINGDOM** and be shielded from it all. You are the light and the salt. You contain the answer. You will demonstrate My Word with POWER.

POWER AND ABILITY that you cannot even conceive of, but I will enlighten you.

The world—your friends, neighbors, fellow workers, and acquaintances will seek you out, because in you is the HOPE of all humanity.

You have prayed for centuries for **MY KINGDOM** to come on earth as it is in Heaven. Some of you sensed the importance of this prayer and some did not. It was repeated by rote without understanding. Even those who have repeated without understanding have contributed to its fulfillment. It is **MY WORD** spoken aloud that has power—*coming from you*.

The fulfillment of that prayer is upon you. Enter into **MY KINGDOM** with power and confidence.

Within your midst (MY BODY), I have set some groups with various assignments.

You are a part of my body with various functions. If your larger group is a hand, then smaller groups of the whole are fingers and one group is an opposing thumb. The thumb is seemingly set against the other fingers. Because of this, the hand is capable of strong grip. Do not despise the thumb group. Embrace them for I have ordained it. Grip is one of the major functions of *MY HAND.*

I have ordained that some groups among you are equipped to bring thousands into new birth. Others are to nurture the new borns into adulthood. (This growth must now be accelerated because of the time.)

Do not be prideful of numbers of new borns in your midst. Neither be envious of the groups I have ordained for this cause. Remember that I am El Shaddai, the big breasted God. I have ordained some groups for nurturing. Measure your effectiveness not in numbers of new borns, but in mature Kingdom Dwellers.

Many fellowships and sheep have become content---even dead. *I am re igniting desires and dreams long dormant.* I am putting an urgent, compelling need into many to obtain my ultimate presence and power. From all fellowships, *I am bringing life from ashes.* You have made this possible by declaring **"Thy Kingdom Come"** for these hundreds of years. **It is NOW, My Father's good pleasure to give you *THE KINGDOM***

ACKNOWLEDGEMENTS

I would like to acknowledge **_Lady Tracy Russell_** for providing inspiration for this book. She is First Lady of Revelation Knowledge Bible Church (RKBC) of Pinson Alabama, where her husband Reverend Larry Russell is Shepherd. The flock respectfully calls her _Lady Love;_ and that is not without good cause. She asked me a question one night and I gave her a partial answer. Lady Tracy, this is the rest of the story.

Rev. David Knight, Sr. was Pastor of the First United Methodist church in East Stone Gap, Virginia at a time when I was so hungry for more of the Lord. Pastor Dave and his wife, **_Judy_** introduced my wife, our three daughters and me to the Baptism in the Holy Spirit and provided an atmosphere where we could grow spiritually. Rev. Dave and Judy reside in Big Stone Gap, Virginia.

Apostle/Pastor Dennis Arnold was the first person that the Lord used to prophesy to me that I would be writing books. He also taught me that I should be "hearing the voice of God continually." Thanks Apostle Dennis. Apostle Arnold is pastor and founder of Revival Central Training and Equipping Center in Alabaster, Alabama. He is author of the book "LEFT TO DIE;" his life story. He is also an anointed singer and has recorded a number of albums.

I wish to acknowledge **_Joseph Sturgeon_** for introducing me to the concept of the treasures of darkness. Joseph is a talented preacher and teacher of the gospel of the Kingdom. Joseph teaches prophetic classes at his home in central Alabama and elsewhere. He has a powerful healing ministry as well as being a powerfully anointed SEER and author of ***"TREASURES OF DARKNESS" Chronicles of a Seer*** that is available on Amazon and at local Bible Book stores.

A shout out must go to **Prophetess Victoria Werneth** of World Outreach Center, who spoke a word of prophesy from the Lord to me in August 2011 saying that I would be writing books. These words from the Lord were confirmation of what He was already speaking to my spirit. Prophetess Victoria, this is the first of many.

ENDORSEMENTS

Loved it! Get ready to be transformed! Get ready to soar high in the heavens, as revelation from God explodes on the inside! For such as a time as this! **Victoria Werneth**

CHAPTER 1

THY KINGDOM COME

ADULTS ONLY

THE MYSTERIES OF THE KINGDOM SERIES OF BOOKS
IS WRITTEN FOR THE SPIRITUALLY MATURE CHRISTIAN
WHO <u>MUST</u> KNOW MORE;
WHO HAS A GREAT GNAWING ON THE INSIDE
TO UNDERSTAND;
WHO ETERNALLY CRAVES DEEPER INTIMACY
WITH JESUS;
WHO'S MIND IS SWIRLING, TRYING TO CATCH UP WITH
THE TREMENDOUS OUTPOURING OF
REVELATION FROM GOD INTO
HIS/HER SPIRIT FOR, THIS
GENERATION.

If you can identify with any of the above statements, then you have been invited/called by The Lord to be an active participant in a great *PARADIGM* shift in the Body of Christ orchestrated by God The Father, Himself. This shift is greater than any shift in the history of the Church or the history of Israel. Mysteries are being revealed that have been hidden *for* us since before the Creation. The prophets of old longed to see them revealed, but could not, even though they prophesied about them. The Apostles and prophets of the early church wrote about them without having the full understanding of their own *inspired* words. This generation in general *and you and I* in particular are beginning to receive a new kind of revelation from Holy Spirit. This is a *special category of revelation* that reveals mysteries of the Kingdom of God that have been hidden *for us* until this generation.

If after having read the above introduction, you do not feel a divine burn in your spirit—a fire in your belly—a knowing that says, "That's it, that's it, that's *ME,*" please do not proceed any further. Just disregard it. It is not for you—at least at this time. However, if by now you are bristling with anticipation by all means jump in head first!

The secret things belong unto the LORD our God: but those things which are <u>revealed</u> belong unto us and to our children for ever, that we may do all the words of this law. Deut. 29:29

By the power of Holy Spirit we are going to plumb the depths of mysteries of God. We will build precept upon precept and line upon line. We will take Holy Spirit by the hand and soar to heights with Him that we have never dreamed possible. We will see things and witness events in the heavenliest that defy explanation, as did the Apostle Paul; as did John The Revelator; as did Moses.

We are going far beyond parables, proverbs, and dark cryptic sayings. We are going into the realm of the Spirit that has *no natural counterpart* that can be used as an illustration. So hold on to your hat, fasten your seatbelt, and prepare for the most amazing ride of your life.

Jesus admonished us to pray, "….Thy Kingdom come, thy will be done on Earth as it is in Heaven." What if that prayer is answered in the affirmative? What does it look like? How will it begin? *It has already begun.* It is being birthed in those who are not just watching and praying, but those who are yearning and burning. If you are still reading this, it has begun in *YOU*. *YOU* are a chosen vessel.

The learning curve is very steep because the time is now; therefore we are going to leap into this study fast and furiously. *You don't want it any other way. You have waited long enough. You have decided to follow the admonition of Paul that he wrote to the Philippians in chapter three:*

Not as though I had already attained, either were already perfect: but I follow after, if that I may apprehend that for which also I am apprehended of Christ Jesus. Brethren, I count not myself to have apprehended: but this one thing I do, forgetting those things which are behind, and reaching forth unto those things which are before, I press toward the mark for the prize of the high calling of God in Christ Jesus. Let us therefore, as many as be perfect, be thus minded: and if in anything ye be otherwise minded, God shall reveal even this unto you. Nevertheless, whereto we have already attained, let us walk by the same rule, let us mind the same thing.

We are like a paratrooper bailing out of an airplane. We have arrived over the jump zone. Please do not proceed any further—do not jump until you pray for the ears of your understanding to be opened to hear what Holy Spirit is saying in the following pages. *{You will be taught an even more accurate way to pray this prayer a bit later.}* From the git-go let me give you God's phone number in case of emergency. Store it on your cell phone on speed dial and put it on your rolodex. It is *Je*remiah 33:3 *"Call unto me, and I will answer thee, and shew thee great and mighty* **(HIDDEN)** *things, which thou knowest not."*

OKAY, JUMP!!

You and I are disciples of Jesus Christ and thus the following statement by our Lord is for us.

And he said unto them**,** *Unto you it is given to know the mystery of the kingdom of God: but unto them that are without, all these things are done in parables: That seeing they may see, and not perceive; and hearing they may hear, and not understand; lest at any time they should be converted, and their sins should be forgiven them.* Mark 4:11-12

The mysteries of the Kingdom of God can neither be taught nor discovered; they must be revealed. The best that those of us who are teachers can do is to lead you in the right direction that you might be able to position yourself in a place where Holy Spirit can reveal them to you personally. We can lead you by the hand just so far, but there is a point where we must let go and allow you to lay hold onto who Jesus is and to be completely engulfed in the light of the understanding of who He is.

If we as the disciples of Jesus are given to know the Mysteries of the Kingdom of God, what is the mechanism by which that is carried out? How has God equipped man to enable him to acquire this knowledge? Because you are mature seekers and searchers, I am not going to dwell on things that you already have nailed down in your spiritual understanding; but rather move on to things that you may not as yet understand.

As Holy Spirit begins to reveal Mysteries of the Kingdom to you, I promise you that you will be confronted by the minions of the Kingdom of Darkness that will tell you, *"Ah, that's just your imagination."*

Let's quench that fiery dart before he can get it out of his quiver. We'll take a close look at this thing we call our *IMAGINATION*.

That is the first precept that we will lay down is fundamental, and I believe it to be a vital teaching from God's Word for today's Christian. Please read and reread it prayerfully. I trust Holy Spirit to reveal to you what I cannot with mere words on a page. He must bring them to life in you.

GREEN PEARS

Do you like pears? I was in a supermarket a few days ago and there were several varieties of pears on display so I bought a bag. They're not like apples—they have a completely different texture. When you bite into one you can feel the gritty texture, unless it is really mushy ripe. Apples, on the other hand, are usually smoother. I personally like canned or frozen pears better than fresh ones. Some of you may prefer pears over apples.

I was raised up in a coal camp. It was in the Blue Ridge Mountains of Virginia—On the Trail of The Lonesome Pine. [*The Trail of the Lonesome Pine* is a book written by one of our local citizens, John Fox, Jr. The longest, continuously running out door drama by the same name is located in Big Stone Gap.] In 1958, my family bought twenty-five acres of land and we moved out of the coal camp. My parents dream since I can remember was to move out of "the camp" and to get away from "the store." You remember the kind of Company Store that Tennessee Ernie Ford owed his soul to in his song.

On this property were lots of fruit trees that had been neglected for years. We had several kinds of apple, wild cherry, paw-paw, and pear trees. We even had two trees that were a cross between an apple and a pear. They were weird.

ENGLAND SWINGS

When my wife, Norma was pregnant with our first daughter Lesia, she *CRAVED green pears*—not ripe ones, but *green ones.*

We lived in East Suffolk County England. Do you realize how hard it is to find green pears in England during winter? Fresh fruit was hard to find, but *green pears* were nearly impossible. We lived in Mildenhall. Market day in Mildenhall was on Wednesday. I often walked the mile or so from Heath Caravan Court where we lived on Pitch #10 to the open air market, desperately hoping that I could find *green pears.* Believe it or not, occasionally, I was successful. I felt like the fearless hunter coming home with the kill.

Ladies, did any of you ever crave anything strange when you were pregnant with one of your children? What was it? The old joke is pickles and ice cream. When my daughter, Kim was pregnant with my grandson, Casey she craved chalk and dirt. Ugh! She teaches fourth grade now. Maybe that chalk was a precursor. I don't know.

Gals, why does that happen, anyway? Is your body really screaming, "I am low on a certain nutrient or I'm missing that nutrient?" *Or is it just your imagination?* Could you see, smell, taste and feel whatever it was that you craved. Did you ever crave something, but didn't know what it was? Boy, I know that had to be miserable for you *and* Hubby.

How did Norma's body know that the nutrients that it needed were in *green pears? I don't know.*

HUSBANDS, I KNOW, you remember when Momma craved something. No matter what time of night or day it was she was going to get it. She was not going to be denied, especially with the first child, right? Have any of you ever had to go out in bad weather; snow storms, hurricanes, tornados or whatever to get what Momma needed? Ain't nobody gonna get no peace 'til Momma is satisfied, right?

THE OTHER SIDE OF THE COIN

Snooshel's grocery truck came round one day a week to Heath Caravan Court. You knew when it arrived because it played music, similar to an ice-cream truck. That music was nauseating when you were **normal**. Norma was not normal. In the first weeks, she got so sick hearing that sound. However, Snooshel's Cokes were 1 and 1. (One shilling and one pence—about 15 cents.) [Another craving was for Cokes] We scrimped to save enough money for Norma to have a Coke once a week and also a Shillin' for her bus fare into base on payday.

That was a long, long time ago in a galaxy far, far away.

How in the world can a ***sound*** cause someone to throw up? Maybe, the morning sickness thing is the opposite of the craving, I don't know; any ideas, Ladies?

MIRAGES

At one time or another all of us have seen an old movie where someone is stranded in the desert with no water. He walks a while then crawls. His face is blistered and his lips are parched. Finally, off in the distance he sees an oasis with cool water aplenty and trees for shade from the scorching sun. You and I know that it is not real. We know that it is a mirage. *It's all in his imagination.*

Psalms 42:1 says *"As the deer pants after the water brooks, so pants my soul after thee, O God."*

Almost all advertisement relies on the consumer's imagination. "WHEATIES, THE BREAKFAST OF CHAMPIONS"[1] Your favorite baseball, football, or basketball Champion eats Wheaties, so your imagination says, "If I eat Wheaties, I too will be a Champion.

Young children have vivid imaginations. Many times they have imaginary friends or pets that they play with.

What in the world does craving green pears and desert mirages and Wheaties have to do with the Lord, anyway?

Usually when we say, "It's just your imagination," we mean that it isn't real. It is like the mirage of the oasis in the desert. If we limit our understanding of the imagination to just something not real, we have grossly underestimated its purpose and power. *The imagination is the interface between our human spirit and Holy Spirit. It is part of our spirit man.* Because it is part of the spirit of man; it is powerful; however we must keep it in line with the will and word of God.

Your imagination is just like the modem between your home computer and the internet; both are two-way data exchanges—input and output.

We have seen with Norma's Green Pears the input into our imagination from our five senses in the natural. We looked at examples of the enemy whispering lies into our imagination. Once you can wrap the arms of your spirit around this concept you will discover many scriptures where angels and Holy Spirit Himself influences our imagination. Let's look at just one example. It has to do with the most important thing of all—our soul salvation.

No man can come to me, except the Father which hath sent me draw him: and I will raise him up at the last day. John 6:44

Our Heavenly Father didn't open a window in Heaven and yell to us to come to Jesus. He "drew" our spirit man to Jesus by way of our **imagination.**

POWER AND IMPORTANCE

Without our imagination, literature would be pretty useless. Reading *"Alice in Wonderland"* would be nothing without our imagination. We all remember the Mad Hatter, and the Queen of Hearts. I'll bet that your imagination just kicked in and gave you a mental image of those two characters. But, never mind literature; *without imagination, we couldn't even have LANGUAGE.*

In 1871 Charles Darwin's *The Descent of Man* was published. In it Darwin cites a quote by philologist Horne Tooke and adds his correction.

"As Horne Tooke, one of the founders of the noble science of philology observes, language is an art, like brewing or baking; but writing would

have been a better simile. It certainly is not a true instinct, for every language has to be learnt. It differs, however, widely from all ordinary arts, for man has an instinctive tendency to speak, as we see in the babble of our young children; whilst no child has an instinctive tendency to brew, bake, or write. Moreover, no philologist now supposes that any language has been deliberately invented; it has been slowly and unconsciously developed by many steps."[2]

I suppose that each of us will cede the point that thought is behind the words we speak. If thought precedes speech, a number of follow-up questions arise; such as how much and what kind of thought; how simple or complex is this thought process?

What is thought, anyway? You can't see it, touch it, or feel it; yet you know that it is real. This is the area where we make a distinction between the brain and the mind. We as Christians add yet another dimension to this mix. We believe that our essence is spirit. The core of our being is referred to as our spirit man. The spirit of man is also capable of thought and communication; communication with our mind and the Spirit of God. As this study declares, the imagination is that part of our spirit man that interfaces with the Spirit of God and is hard wired to our soul or mind.

The fossil record reveals that humans have had imagination from the git-go. Evidence of the manufacturing and manipulation of tools that required several steps to fashion from various materials that sometimes had to be collected in distant locals appear suddenly in the fossil record; only with human remains.[3,4] Some of these tools, or weapons were carefully crafted into projectile points. This process required much more cognitive ability than did finding a use for flakes randomly broken off of a core stone. These processes required imagination, reasoning, and purpose both to learn the methods of manufacturing, best materials available for a given tool, and the ability to use the tool for utilitarian purposes, fishing, hunting, or fighting. Language along with its symbolic thinking and imagination was absolutely necessary for these techniques to be passed from one to another and from generation to generation.

When it comes to symbolism, humans have abilities that are exponentially beyond anything that could ever be expected from the most sophisticated animal, past or present. The fossil record reveals a "Cultural Big Bang" when man first appeared on the scene. Tool technology exploded and changed the culture of these people tremendously, yet at the same time another demonstration of symbolic thinking popped up suddenly. That is the making of jewelry. An argument has been posited that tool making, born of necessity became gradually more sophisticated. Fossil records show an explosion with the advent of man rather than an evolution of these abilities. The argument for necessity being the pressure to drive evolution of cognitive abilities that is needed for tool making cannot be used for the creating of jewelry. Jewelry has no intrinsic or utilitarian value. Jewelry represents something intangible. It is symbolic and requires symbolic cognitive abilities to make and to appreciate. It requires the image of God. We still wear jewelry to represent various religious concepts such as crosses, crucifixes, stars of David, St. Christopher medals, or wedding bands. Jewelry is often used to decorate ourselves for various purposes. The purpose may be to attract a mate, or to ward off an enemy. Some of the oldest human fossils ever found are in caves in France. These sites reveal more shell fish used for jewelry than for food.[5] If she had to choose between food and a pretty piece of jewelry, I think my wife would choose the ring or bracelet every time. Hey, I think it makes her look pretty good, too.

The number one tenet of the evolutionary paradigm is that every organism must change very slowly, step by step over vast amounts of time due to random mutations caused by environmental pressures that prove to be beneficial to the organism. This defines evolution. Darwin's statement about language presupposes the evolution paradigm to be true. If it were true, it would logically follow that language did indeed slowly develop rather than its having been *deliberately invented*. It disappoints me to think that the learned Charles Darwin would use this fallacy of logic. He is stooping to the use of a rhetorical question. When he says, "....no philologist now supposes," he is assuming that the answer is a foregone conclusion—it just makes sense. The reason that rhetorical questions are not accepted in any logical debate is that the premise is often faulty. If the philologist does not concur with the premise that the evolution of man paradigm is the correct view, then there is no reason that he cannot conceive of the notion that language could have emerged some other way, including having been *deliberately invented*.

From the Darwinian perspective, one is compelled to assume that human speech gradually evolved. Of all of the attributes of man that give the evolutionary worldview tremendous challenges, this thing that we call language is its greatest "thorn in the side." It simply refuses to fall in line with that thinking. It is beyond stubborn. Can you imagine that?

PORTALS INTO OUR IMAGINATION

Let's take a close look at those five I/O portals.

!. Our Mind (Soul)
2. Evil Spirits
3. Angelic Spirits
4. Our Spirit Man
5. Holy Spirit

Our own mind (soul) has dialog with our *imagination.* The imagination is a major part of our Spirit Man. When we were saved and became a new creature, our imagination was regenerated, also. Paul tells us in Romans 12:1-2 to be transformed by the renewing of our mind. Our self talk according to our self image (imagination) affects us either positively or negatively. Solomon declared in Proverbs 23:7 *For as he thinks in his heart, so is he:*

Much of the input into our imagination from our soul originates with the *"sense gates."* This refers to our five senses. We will discuss the sense gates in a bit more detail in Chapter Two.

Demonic principalities and powers endeavor to speak to our *imagination.*
Demonic beings sent to deter the saint from his assignment from the Lord.

When any one hears the word of the kingdom, and understands it not, then cometh the **wicked one***, and catches away that which was sown in his heart. This is he which received seed by the way side.* Matt. 13:19

Do you remember when you were born again, forgiven of your sins. You were so excited. Then the next day, the wicked one tried to steal that seed—that word from your heart. He whispered, "You weren't saved, that was *just your imagination."*

When you were baptized with the Holy Spirit, it wasn't long 'til ole Slewfoot whispered in your ear again, "Ah, praying in tongues—that's nothing but gibberish—it's *just in your imagination."*

Angelic beings sent from God desire to talk with us. Holy messengers sent from God to minister to the saints; guardian angels, warring angels, and even archangels.

Can you remember seeing cartoons with a little imp on one shoulder of Daffy Duck and an angel on the other whispering in his ears?

Our Spirit Man before salvation is full of mischief, carnal, and subject to the law of sin and death. Upon receiving the free gift of salvation, the spirit man is reconciled to God by Christ Jesus and is subject to the law of life. We then begin what some consider a lifelong struggle to make our spirit man which is aligned with Holy Spirit to have preeminence in our life. Our soul must be brought under subjection to our spirit man and in turn our flesh made to obey the oracles of God through the renewing of our mind. Although the renewing of the mind and the aligning of the imagination with the Holy Spirit is a process, it is not intended to be a lifetime struggle. Often the church has propagated the concept that dedicated and committed Christians are *"Ever learning, but never able to come to the knowledge of the truth."* We should never characterize our processes of having our mind renewed and our imagination properly aligned using this warning from 2 Timothy 3:7. Paul, writing to his son in the Spirit, Timothy, is not speaking of Christians, but those who attempt to put on the guise of Christians but in reality have never actually received the truth of Jesus and His salvation.

The interface between the spirit man and Holy Spirit is our imagination. The revelations, rhema words, edicts, corrections, and admonishments from Holy Spirit are formatted in our imagination and then passed on to the whole of our spirit man to be processed and then to our mind for implementation. Since the imagination is an input/output device, it also processes and formats data from our spirit man to Holy Spirit. One of the "programs" in the imagination that formats the ***output*** of our imagination is our ***Prayer Language***, i.e. praying in tongues. *Likewise the Spirit also helps our infirmities: for we know not what we should pray for as we ought: but the Spirit itself makes intercession for us with groanings which cannot be uttered. And* *he that searches the hearts knows what is the mind of the Spirit, because he makes intercession for the saints **according to the will of God.*** Rom. 8:26-27

Holy Spirit longs to communicate with us via our *imagination*. Prayer is intended to be a <u>dialog</u> between man and God not a monologue. This is just another of the myriad of reasons that Satan has desperately tried to squelch our prayer language from the moment that the Church was launched on the Day of Pentecost. Unfortunately, he has had tremendous success in this arena. Even those of us who acknowledge the authenticity and validly of tongues do not practice the use of that wonderful gift nearly as much as we should. Now that you and I know yet another important purpose of our prayer language, let's agree to be much more vigorous in its use.

EVIL IMAGINATIONS

The multi-billion dollar *porno* industry depends on an unregenerate imagination. Scripture is replete with stern warnings about evil imaginations. We'll look at a few examples.

Because that, when they knew God, they glorified him not as God, neither were thankful; but became vain in their imaginations, and their foolish heart was darkened. Rom. 1:21

For this cause God gave them up unto vile affections: for even their women did change the natural use into that which is against nature: And likewise also the men, leaving the natural use of the woman, burned in their lust one toward another; men with men working that which is unseemly, and receiving in themselves that recompense of their error which was meet. (Homosexuality) Rom. 1:26-27

But I say unto you, That whosoever looks on a woman to lust after her hath committed adultery with her already in his heart. Matt. 5:28

Wow! Jesus considered acts done in the imagination to be equivalent to those done in "reality." Double WOW!

God sure considers it a powerful spiritual force. Just look what He did because of imagination in Genesis chapter eleven.

And the LORD said, Behold, the people is one, and they have all one language; and this they begin to do: and now nothing will be restrained from them, which they have imagined to do.

Let us go down, and there confound their language, that they may not understand one another's speech. So the LORD scattered them abroad from thence upon the face of all the earth: and they left off building the city. Therefore is the name of it called Babel; because the LORD did there confound the language of all the earth: and from thence did the LORD scatter them abroad upon the face of all the earth. Gen. 11:5-9

Napoleon Hill, author of THINK AND GROW RICH proclaimed, "What the mind of man can conceive and believe; he can achieve."[5] *Could that be true?* There have been hundreds of self-help books based on that idea.

But what if you gain the whole world and lose your soul, what would you give in exchange for his soul? Mt 16:26

If you think that confounding languages because of power of the imagination was a big deal, just look at Genesis Chapter six. *The imagination* is so important to God that He destroyed the Earth with the Flood because of evil imagination.

And GOD saw that the wickedness of man was great in the earth, and that every imagination of the thoughts of his heart was only evil continually.

And it repented the LORD that he had made man on the earth, and it grieved him at his heart.

And the LORD said, I will destroy man whom I have created from the face of the earth; both man, and beast, and the creeping thing, and the fowls of the air; for it repents me that I have made them.

But Noah found grace in the eyes of the LORD. Gen. 6:5-8

Well, I think we've made our case that the imagination is vastly important in our spiritual walk both to us and our Lord. It is obvious that it is a powerful spiritual force and that there is a tug-o-war going on between the Kingdom of Darkness and the Kingdom of Light for its control. It is crucial that we as Christians yield our imagination to the Lord and make sure it is aligned with God. Our Lord has made us the gatekeeper and given us the wherewithal to be victorious.

(For the weapons of our warfare are not carnal, but mighty through God to the pulling down of strong holds;) Casting down imaginations, and every high thing that exalts itself against the knowledge of God, and bringing into captivity every thought to the obedience of Christ; 2 Cor. 10:4-5

Paul, here is speaking to Christians, you and me. He is saying that we may have strong holds, vain imaginations, and unholy thoughts but that they can be brought into proper alignment with the will of God. Verse five infers that our imagination can be aligned with the Kingdom of Darkness and must be brought into captivity or into control and obedience to Jesus.

It is critical at this juncture to make a definitive statement. We are not talking about some NEW AGE delusion. On the contrary, the aim and focus of this work is just the opposite. For far too long the Bride of Christ has allowed the Kingdom of Darkness to rob us of our abilities and authority that we have through Jesus. Often the true power of God has been dismissed by the Church because Satan has counterfeited it. We tend to throw the baby out with the bath. Dear brothers and sisters that should not be. This ploy of Satan finds its ultimate example in the coming Antichrist. He will be a counterfeit of the true Christ—Jesus. Part of the manifestation of the Kingdom of God is to take back that which the enemy has stolen and reclaim it for ourselves.

On top of what you already know and are walking in as a mature Christian we have added another dimension to your understanding of who you are in Christ. Let's recap:

- The Imagination is part of your spirit man
- The Imagination is the interface between your spirit and Holy Spirit
- The Imagination is a very powerful force in your life
- God sees the Imagination as being powerful
- Satan tries to squelch and minimize the Godly Imagination
- Satan tries to corrupt the Imagination
- There are spiritual weapons that can correct corrupt imaginations

Now, let's stand upon these new precepts and go even further into the realm of the Imagination. First we will look into ***how we can effectively*** cast down those vain imaginations and bring every though into captivity and in alignment with the Word of God. Then we will learn ***how to apply*** this to our flowing in our ministry giftings and lastly we will use all of this spiritual information to walk in that arena of Mysteries of the Kingdom for this generation.

CHAPTER 2

IMAGINATION PLUMBED DEEPER

Whom shall he teach knowledge? and whom shall he make to understand doctrine? them that are weaned from the milk, and drawn from the breasts. For precept must be upon precept, precept upon precept; line upon line, line upon line; here a little, and there a little: Isa. 28:9-10

We are going to go farther and *plumb the depths of the imagination* a bit deeper. We'll stand on the shoulders of the previous teaching that ended with…

(For the weapons of our warfare are not carnal, but mighty through God to the pulling down of strongholds;) Casting down imaginations, and every high thing that exalts itself against the knowledge of God, and bringing into captivity every thought to the obedience of Christ; 2 Cor.10:4-5

If your experience has been similar to mine, you have heard that scripture preached and taught numerous times, but there was not much by way of instruction as to what those spiritual weapons may look like or how to apply them. We'll not stop with just acknowledging that spiritual weapons exist, but we'll press on to explore a few of those weapons of spiritual warfare that can pull down strongholds, cast down those evil imaginations and bring them into obedience to Christ. Does that sound good to you?

BROKENHEARTED

It would be remiss of me indeed to present a study of the imagination and not address one of the greatest challenges to the serious child of God in that area. Of all of the areas where we need weapons that can cast down vain imaginations it is in the area that I have labeled "Brokenhearted." It involves the input from your soul. A proper study of this subject would require a completely separate work. Space does not allow for that here, however at least some consideration must be given. Before we investigate the spiritual weapons that we can use to cast down these and other vain imaginations and strongholds of the enemy, let's look for a moment at broken heartedness. Dear reader, if you are a victim of this debilitating problem, please do not hesitate to appropriate all of the weapons for yourself.

The proper order of hierarchy within the human being is spirit, soul, and then body. There is always a tug-of-war between the three for preeminence. Your soul has tremendous input into your spirit via your imagination. As we learned from Romans 12:2 the transformation of the mind is a process. While that process is going on, there will be negative inputs caused by a variety of sources.

Just for a moment let's liken our mind/soul to an acre of very fertile soil. Most of us up until we were born again and began to associate with other believers, allowed just about anyone to toss any kind of seed into our little acre. Unfortunately in some fellowships, bad seeds continue to be thrown into the fertile soul of the babes in Christ. That should not be. Some seed was thrown into it by those whom we had little or no control over, such as parents, teachers, and other authority figures. Many of those seeds were very negative. Whether they were good seeds or bad, they have been growing all of this time, and now we are praying for a *crop failure.*

When a person is born again, his spirit is regenerated and he becomes a new creature in Christ Jesus. However, he must mature and be renewed and transformed in his mind. Evidence of bad seeds growing to maturity in the fertile acre of our mind is poor self image (imagination), bad self esteem, and depression; and feelings of unworthiness, uselessness, and inadequacy. You may have been struggling with some of these symptoms ever since you have been a Christian. Therefore the minions of the Kingdom of Darkness tend to harass you more than most with the refrain, *"It's just in your imagination, because you are not worthy of hearing God's voice nor obeying it."* You are very mature in other areas of your Christian walk, but still struggle in this area. I have some tremendous news for you. Just keep reading and praying.

The Psalmist experienced some of those same feelings in Ps.38:8 and 69:20 respectively.

I am feeble and sore broken: I have roared by reason of the disquietness of my heart.

Reproach hath broken my heart; and I am full of heaviness: and I looked for some to take pity, but there was none; and for comforters, but I found none.

Solomon made similar observations in Prov. 15:13 and 17:22.

A merry heart maketh a cheerful countenance: but by sorrow of the heart the spirit is broken.

A merry heart doeth good like a medicine: but a broken spirit drieth the bones.

One way to sum these issues up in one tidy bundle is to call it being brokenhearted. Well, guess what, Jesus came to bind up the brokenhearted; folks just like you. It was prophesied by Isaiah, four hundred and seventy years before Jesus was born.

The Spirit of the Lord GOD is upon me; because the LORD hath anointed me to preach good tidings unto the meek; he hath sent me to bind up the brokenhearted, to proclaim liberty to the captives, and the opening of the prison to them that are bound;

To proclaim the acceptable year of the LORD, and the day of vengeance of our God; to comfort all that mourn; Isa. 61:1-2

Jesus read in the temple:

The Spirit of the Lord is upon me, because he hath anointed me to preach the gospel to the poor; he hath sent me to heal the brokenhearted, to preach deliverance to the captives, and recovering of sight to the blind, to set at liberty them that are bruised, To preach the acceptable year of the Lord. And he closed the book, and he gave it again to the minister, and sat down. And the eyes of all them that were in the synagogue were fastened on him. And he began to say unto them, This day is this scripture fulfilled in your ears. Luke 4:18-21

***Side Note: Jesus stopped reading in mid sentence and rolled the scroll back up. He did not say "...and the day of vengeance of our God; to comfort all that mourn." The time of the fulfillment of that last phrase was not yet.

You as mature men and women of God have heard all of this and embrace it, even though you still struggle. I have told you nothing new. You may feel that you are stuck at your current spiritual level because of these issues. You want to go farther, but you can't because ***you know*** who you are. By the power of Holy Spirit you are going to be released from that prison to rise up toward your higher calling in Christ Jesus. Just hang on a minute longer.

Extreme cases of bad seed sewing are the direct and/or indirect action of demonic forces such as generational curses, infirmities, mental illnesses, multiple personalities, and ***fragmented souls.*** Let's take a look at what that looks like and what our amazing Heavenly Father is ordaining.

Several years ago, I had the honor of knowing a young Methodist pastor who was assigned to a small church in a rural farming community. When he began his ministry there, he was met with opposition from some of the "old guard." After several months of confrontation he attended a men's group that I also attended. He related a story about one of those men that had been giving him such a hard time. This fellow had done something so Christ like that the pastor was forced to realize that the Lord was indeed using this man. That pastor made a statement that I will never forget. He said, "God uses a lot of people that I would never use." He was scolding himself for not seeing Christ in this person before. From that point the pastor and his church were the model of love and mutual appreciation.

Many times I look in the mirror and wonder why in the world our Lord uses the likes of me. If I was God, I wouldn't use me. Thank God I am not Him. I see people with many issues in their life and with fouled up theology still being used mightily by the Lord. Often it is easier to see someone else's errors and shortcomings than our own. The Lord has taught me over the past several years to look beyond the problems and receive what He has for me through that person. That does not mean that I condone those errors or dismiss terrible teaching, but I pray that the Vision of their Imagination be Engulfed in the Light of who Jesus is.

I hear you questioning that precept, "Okay, Fred prove what you just said. Where is the scripture to back it up?" Since this book is for Adults Only, I fully expect you to challenge my assertions. Scripture says to try everything and hold fast to that which is good. I encourage your questioning. I will give you only one scripture as proof however, it is so clear that it alone will suffice.

For the gifts and calling of God are without repentance. Rom. 11:29

Here the Greek word rendered "calling" can also be translated *"invitation."* The Greek word translated "without repentance" in the King James can be translated *"irrevocable"*

The bottom line is that while we can diminish the intensity of the power associated with our gifts and calling, God does not take them away. They are irrevocable. Do you not think that He knew your weaknesses and all of those issues before He gave you those gifts? *Is that good news, or what?* Did I hear a *"Yeah, but!* Fred, you just don't know how messed up I am. I had these horrible things to happen to me when I was a child, and even though I have been a born again believer for many years, I still struggle with this awful mess. It is really bad, but I am working on it by the power of Jesus' name. Can the Lord *really* use me mightily?"

The short answer is, *"YES!"*

The Lord had been dealing with me on these issues for a number of years before I ever heard the phrase *"Fragmented Soul."* It may be that YOU dear reader have a fragmented soul that you are dealing with. Let's see, okay?

In his book, TIME TO DEFEAT THE DEVIL, (Charisma House 2011) internationally recognized Apostle and Prophet, Dr. Charles D. "Chuck" Pierce writes on page 207:

*Many leaders who have never dealt with **fragmentation of their soul** bring only a piece of what God wants into a movement. Many even carry bipolar structures into the ministry. There is a side of that bipolar, fragmented soul that the anointing works through. Many in the religious world do not understand how the anointing can work in the bipolar realm. The anointing will flow through one portion of the redeemed personality of an individual, while the demonic subdues itself in a portion that is not sanctified. Then the demonic comes alive at an opportune time and works to rise up and create confusion.*

You may be saying, "You have identified that which causes me to be reluctant to move forward. I certainly do not want to be like so many other leaders." The good news for you and me comes as Dr. Pierce continues with a prophecy.

We judge individuals based upon their wholeness as opposed to how God is working through their fragmentation. I think we must get a handle on this as we move forward in this next season. The next great move of God will be filled with fragmented individuals seeking wholeness, not whole individuals ready to advance.

His love searches out what He knit together. Previously we discussed how our spirit, soul, and body are all meant to be sanctified. We might have begun life with fragmentation of soul, but by His Spirit transforming our spirit man, our end can be greater than our beginning.[1]

The bottom line is that you, by your own abilities are not worthy to be used mightily by the Lord. None of us are. Our righteousness is as filthy rags. The very best that we can do is not enough. However, we—you and I are the righteousness of God in

Christ Jesus. We may have a fragmented soul that we are dealing with, but not only *can* He still use us but He wants to use a bunch of folks like us to accomplish great things in His Kingdom. Hallelujah! Those of you who have been hanging back "gird up your loins" and come with us.

One of those weapons of warfare for the tearing down of vain imaginations is found in Hebrews chapter five.

But strong meat belongs to them that are of full age, even those who by reason of use have their senses exercised to discern both good and evil. Heb. 5:14

This is a good opportunity to talk a bit about the five sense gates; touch, smell, hearing, sight, and taste. Do you remember my wife, Norma who craved green pears? She could smell, feel, taste, and see those green pears because her body screamed for them. When the grocery truck came by, she became nauseated just hearing that music. The man crawling in the hot desert could see and taste water and feel the breeze. Did you know that if you have your senses exercised that you can discern Holy Spirit as he is ministering?

As we mature as the writer of Hebrews says we should be exercising our five senses to discern both good and evil. The five natural senses are a part of our flesh—our physical bodies and are connected to our soul; our mind; our emotions. Our soul in turn is connected to our spirit man via our imagination. Stay with me a minute; these are an important couple of paragraphs. For many of you, as it was with me when Holy Spirit began teaching me these things, I had to unlearn a lot of concepts that I was taught and had learned in error. I must reiterate some concepts. Okay?

Many of us were taught that after salvation that one of the battles for the rest of our lives would be to constantly killing "the flesh." We want to be spiritual minded and think that to do so we must destroy the flesh. Scripture says that we have been crucified (killed) with Christ and have been raised with Him as a new Creature. Rather than constantly trying to kill the flesh, why not do as scripture tells us and bring the flesh into proper alignment with our soul which is being brought into proper alignment with our spirit man (renewing of our mind and casting down vain imaginations); which is in alignment with Holy Spirit. That is exactly what Hebrews 5:14 is telling us.

STOP for a minute and ask Holy Spirit to teach you how to begin this process. One of the purposes that Jesus sent Holy Spirit to us was to be a teacher. Take as long as you need before proceeding. (Don't try to rush through just to read these pages; but rather ponder and apply each precept that you can agree with to your life before moving on. If you never read another word of this work, but allowed Holy Spirit to apply the preceding principles to your life, then this effort will have been successful.)

You may have already started this process without realizing exactly what it was. This is going to be a nutty analogy, but here goes. Do you remember learning to ride a bicycle? Remember how awkward you were and how hard it was to keep your balance? After several trials and failures, you finally mastered it. It became "second nature." Your brain actually rewired itself and created new pathways to control your muscles for bike riding. You may not have ridden a bike for many years, but if you got on one right now, you could ride the first try. The same is true when exercising your senses for discernment.

The five sense gates are also "wired" to the brain. They collect raw data from the environment and send it to the brain for processing. The mind interrupts these signals. As we become more spiritual minded, our soul adds a spiritual dimension to these interruptions. We learned earlier these five sense gates provide input via our soul into the imagination and communicate with Holy Spirit.

He in turn teaches, enlightens, and transforms our mind. It is almost as though there are five spiritual senses that correspond to the natural ones. With practice the connection between them becomes more and more solidified. Soon, what we see with our eyes; hear with our ears, feel, or smell will immediately be reflected into the spirit. Seeing and hearing in the spirit through these sense gates will become "second nature."

Holy Spirit will set us up with daily encounters to minister to people in ways that you never dreamed possible. This is ordained of God. This is gifts from God for you and me.

Touch

For she said within herself, If I may but touch his garment, I shall be whole. Mt 9:21

Laying on of Hands is probably the best known example of the Spiritual use of the sense of touch. Volumes have been penned on this topic. We find it throughout the pages of scripture. It is used in anointing for gifts, priests, kings, apostles, prophets, baptism in Holy Spirit, and the list goes on and on.

In chapter six of Hebrews, the author considers the doctrine of laying on of hands to be basic along with repentance, and faith toward God and the various baptisms, and the resurrection of the dead.

Apostle Luke writes in Acts chapter eight that Simon saw that the Holy Spirit was given by the laying on of the hands of the Apostles that he offered to buy this great ability. Ole Simon had to have his vain imagination brought into alignment with Holy Spirit, but even he saw how awesome this ability was. He wanted to purchase that which was freely given as a benefit of his salvation. Simon was willing to pay good money for this empowerment, yet much of The Church today ignores it and refuses to accept it as doctrine. That should not be.

Allow me to take a moment and relate a short story that happened to me some time ago. I was involved in an inner healing ministry session with a young man in his late twenties. I was leading him in several short prayers. He repeated the prayers after me. There came a time in the session when we asked Father God if there was anyone that he needed to forgive. He heard Father God tell him that he needed to forgive a former girlfriend that he had lived with for five years. He had to forgive her for rejection (or at least what he perceived as rejection). When he called her name in his prayer of forgiveness, the hair on both of my arms seemed to stand at attention. Immediately, I knew that there was some demonic presence associated with this young lady. I had never met that young man before that day and have never met the woman that he referred to. I continued to lead him in these prayers of forgiveness as the Lord revealed them to him, but simultaneously I was silently asking Holy Spirit what this feeling meant. Holy Spirit revealed to me that there this young lady was involved with the spirit of witchcraft, control, and manipulation. Holy Spirit also forbad me to mention it to this young man at this time, but I must allow him to self discover it with the guidance of Holy Spirit.

We finished this portion of the session in about another half hour and began investigating doors that may have been open in his life to allow sin to enter. One of the doors that we look for is the door to the occult. When he asked Jesus if there was a door to the occult open in his life, Holy Spirit immediately gave him a vision of this former girlfriend. He related that he never saw obvious manifestations of witchcraft from her, but he often wondered if she were putting curses on him in his sleep. He was able to forgive her for this and renounce all soul ties with the occult. He asked Jesus to close that door and to seal it with His blood.

Holy Spirit used one of my five senses, the sense of touch or feeling in this case to direct my attention to the primary reason in the mind of God for this inner healing session with this young man. The other matters, important as they were, were secondary with respect to this hindrance in his spiritual life.

Empathic Pain

Kathie Walter shared about how *God uses empathetic pain to speak to her while ministering to people.* Now this is different than others which I have experienced, where when you are ministering to others you might develop a pain in a body part, and then ask the person if they have a back ache or shoulder pain and they would say yes. You pray for healing and instantly they are healed and the momentary pain you felt is totally gone. In a sense it is kind of a Word of Knowledge about what needs healing. The Lord had given Kathie additional revelation. She experienced pain in her shoulders while ministering to one woman and she said that speaks of religious yokes and false burdens. As she addressed these spiritual bondages the woman was totally delivered and the pain immediately left. www.kathiewalterministry.com

One of the more unusual instances was when Kathie said she was feeling pain in the back of her legs like in the upper calf and lower hamstring area. She said this speaks of striving. She had another lady come and lay hands on the woman who was receiving ministry. I watched the lady receiving prayer totally collapse and go through a major deliverance as Kathie broke the ***bondages of striving and performance off her life***.

Two of my dear friends, Apostle James and Prophetess Victoria Werneth of www.christianinternationalcenter.net, report similar experiences with empathetic pain. They testify that they have never had this happen that God didn't heal the person who had the real pain. One of Apostle James' favorite quotes is, "What God reveals; He heals."

With these examples we are speaking of a *"point of need"* gift to be used immediately by the minister. More than that what we are studying is being able to exercise our senses. Let's take a look at the "Office" of the empathic person. This is found in Romans chapter twelve. This is one of the gifts from Father God—an office rather than a gift of the Holy Spirit.

Empathy

Rejoice with them that do rejoice, and weep with them that weep. Rom 12:15

Both the concept of empathy and of sympathy comes from this verse. A surface reading of Rom. 12:15 leaves us with the suggestion that we should "feel" for others and their plight; their struggles and their successes. Although this is true, if you have been given this gifting, those few words from Holy Spirit penned by Paul speak volumes. This is one of the Treasure of Darkness**.** The depth of it is hidden to the casual observer, but becomes crystal clear to the recipient of this gifting or office.

I will go before thee, and make the crooked places straight: I will break in pieces the gates of brass, and cut in sunder the bars of iron:

*And I will give thee the **treasures of darkness**, and hidden riches of secret places, that thou mayest know that I, the LORD, which call thee by thy name, am the God of Israel.* Isa 45:2-3

*** Important note to the Teacher or Pastor: While it is commendable to admonish every Christian to exhibit a measure of EMPATHY and SYMPATHY, just remember that it is a gifting/an office that individuals walk in. Obviously everyone does not have this gifting. If you have this gifting and as a result insist that everyone else have the same measure as you, you will create a very confused and frustrated group of Christians. If God has not given them this gifting, they cannot walk in it.

If you walk in this gifting, God The Father has given you the capacity to be in the other person's skin; to actually feel what he/she is feeling whether elated or depressed, happy or sad.

And whether one member suffer, all the members suffer with it; or one member be honored, all the members rejoice with it. Now ye are the body of Christ, and members in particular. 1 Cor. 12:26-27

As an Empath, you epitomize this mandate, without much effort. Before you are anything; you are Empathic.

I am a TREKKIE. Several years ago in the original series of STAR TREK the crew of the Starship Enterprise was on a planet where the people of one race were Total Empaths. When they were in close proximity with anyone, they experienced exactly what that person experienced. If the person had a wound of some kind, the Empath would manifest the same wound. Soon, the victim would be healed. However, the Empath retained the wound. It had been transferred. This was the Empath's life—their reason for being.

Well, as expected one of the crew members of the Starship Enterprise became very ill. Even "Bones" with his beeping cure-all high tech 24th century gadgets couldn't cure this disease. Of course the Empath was prepared to sacrifice her life for the crewmember. The moral issue of allowing one person to die for another was ping-ponged back and forth. The Empath won the argument. She died and the crewmember lived. Hummm, that sounds a little like someone we know.

Brother or Sister Empath, your office is quite similar to the Empaths on that imaginary planet. You don't TRY to do it, you just do it. While you cannot absorb and remove either their problem or their blessing; you can share both.

Jesus is an Empath!!

For we have not an high priest which cannot be touched with the feeling of our infirmities; but was in all points tempted like as we are, yet without sin. Heb 4:1

What then is the goal of your work as and Empath?

You are a Jesus stand-in. You are a temporary substitute for Jesus. Don't start calling me a false teacher, just yet. Doesn't scripture teach that we are to become more like Jesus each day? Aren't we the Body of Christ? Does Jesus dwell inside you and me by His Holy Spirit? You are allowing the Jesus in you to be manifested. However, by your Empathy, you are to wean that person off of yourself as their Jesus Substitute and lead him/her to the next step. They have total access to Jesus and all of the Trinity personally.

A great portion of the Church has unfortunately carried this to the extreme. They contend that The Church as represented by the Priests or other Elders is a permanent substitute for Jesus. They teach that the believer has access to Jesus only through The Church.

*** *CAUTION #1 to the Empath:* *Take care that you do not get bogged down with the depressed person to the point that you cannot bring them to that throne of grace.*

CAUTION #2 to the Empath: *Take care that you and your person in need don't began to ENJOY the arrangement to the point that you are beginning TO PLAY GOD. You cannot handle that position, and that person will soon weaken spiritually. The Church is not capable of playing God, either.*

Sight

And I knew him not: but he that sent me to baptize with water, the same said unto me, Upon whom thou shall see the Spirit descending, and remaining on him, the same is he which baptizes with the Holy Spirit. Joh 1:33

*When Jesus **saw** their faith, he said unto the sick of the palsy, Son, thy sins be forgiven thee.* Mark 2:5

And he said, Unto you it is given to know the mysteries of the kingdom of God: but to others in parables; that seeing they might not see, and hearing they might not understand. Luke 8:10

Jesus therefore answered and said unto them, Verily, verily, I say unto you, The Son can do nothing of himself, but what he seeth the Father doing: for what things soever he doeth, these the Son also doeth in like manner. For the Father loveth the Son, and showeth him all things that himself doeth: and greater works than these will he show him, that ye may marvel. John. 5:19-20

We have often heard this scripture read or quoted in church and nodded of shouted, "Amen!" Many of you were thinking, "Of course he only did what he *saw* His Father do, after all He was the Son of God. Jesus was in perfect obedience to the Father." Here is a question that begs asking: If Jesus is the second person of the Godhead, He is God; why would He have to *see* what the Father is doing in order to do those things? Huummm.

Jesus did nothing as "Son of God." All that He did was as "Son of Man" by the power of Holy Spirit. Whatever method that Father God used to communicate to Jesus must also be available to us; else Jesus could not be our model. Jesus made it very clear that He was sending the Holy Spirit back to indwell believers to enable us to do even greater deeds than He did. So what was the mechanism that Holy Spirit used to communicate the deeds of Father God to Jesus? He did not physically stand alongside of Jesus instructing Him. I submit to you that Jesus' imagination was perfectly in alignment with Father God and therefore Holy Spirit showed (Seer Gifting) these things to the Son of Man and He acted accordingly.

This same line of communication is available to us as we use these spiritual weapons to bring our imagination into alignment, bring every thought under control of our spirit man who is in alignment with Holy Spirit; tear down the demonic strongholds in our lives and erect holy strongholds that are ordained of Father God.

An explanation of how the sense of sight can be exercised to discern spiritual matters would not be complete without at least mentioning the SEER anointing. Many books have been written about this wonderful gift. Seers dream prophetic dreams and see visions. These visions can be open or closed. An open vision is one wherein the Seer sees the vision with his natural eyes and not just in the eye of his spirit (imagination). This is the facet of the Seer anointing that we are addressing in this segment. These people see angels, demons; they see into the heavenly realm, into the circumstances of someone that the Lord wants them to minister to, and often see into future events.

Hearing

He that hath ears to hear, let him hear. Mt. 11:15

We have already studied hearing the voice of God in our spirit man—through our imagination. Now we are considering hearing the audible voice of God, the voice of angels, or other spirit beings. I have found that this skill coupled with the spiritual gift of discernment of spirits is a tool that I would not want to be without when I am ministering inner healing to someone. During the brief interview with the client at the beginning of an inner healing session, I almost always "hear" something that has been said that speaks volumes to me. Immediately I know where Father God wants to go with the session and what He wants to heal and set right in the person's life. From that moment, I can relax and go with the flow of the Holy Spirit and just facilitate the communication between the person receiving ministry and the Trinity of God. God is so good!

Smell

But I have all, and abound: I am full, having received of Epaphroditus the things which were sent from you, an odor of a sweet smell, a sacrifice acceptable, well pleasing to God. Phil. 4:18

And when he had taken the book, the four beasts and four and twenty elders fell down before the Lamb, having every one of them harps, and golden vials full of odors, which are the prayers of saints. Rev. 5:8 Many people report smelling Baby Power or a Sweet Smell at certain times when Holy Spirit is ministering.

Kathie Walter's Ministry has a list of more than one hundred aromas that have spiritual applications. Here are a few of the items on that list. For the whole list visit Kathie on the Internet at www.kathiewaltersministry.com.[2]

Ashes—Burnt up, now clean
Baby powder—Cleanse
Fish, bad—False prophesy
Milk, warm—Getting ready to receive
Ocean—Restless

Taste

*O **taste** and see that the LORD is good: blessed is the man that trusts in him.* Ps 34:8

THE FIVE SENSES IN WORSHIP

When we are involved in worship, especially corporate worship; it is a time when we should be able to engage all five our sense gates to input our imagination and interface with Holy Spirit.

As you mature and begin to flow in the Gifts of the Spirit of God, it is vital that you *exercise your imagination* and keep it in obedience to Christ Jesus and in proper alignment with the will of God because you will be involved closely in the lives of others. Do you get it now? As you exercise your senses—that is as you look for, listen for, feel for, smell for, and taste for the presences of Holy Spirit in any situation, you will begin to discern good and evil. If you have all of your senses on constant alert spiritually, Holy Spirit will draw your attention to where He is at work in the lives of other individuals and other groups. This is part of what Paul was writing about in Romans when he admonished the believers to be Spiritually Minded. Most of the time, we think being Spiritually Minded is living a righteous life and producing the fruits of the Spirit. While this is of course true, being Spiritually Minded goes far beyond that. As members of the Body of Christ, we are expected to use all of our gifts, abilities, and anointings to minister to the rest of the Body as well as to unbelievers. The admonishment to exercise this weapon of spiritual warfare implies that it is an ongoing process.

Be aware that the minions of the Kingdom of Darkness never tire of using the same time worn tactics. It'll be the same song, but the second verse. They may not get very far telling you that your salvation that occurred 10, 20, 30 years ago is "just in your imagination." Your answer is, "Yes it is thank you and my imagination is in alignment with the will of God." Now he will try it in a new area that means so much to you—your gifts and callings from God. Just remember that you are in good company. Satan started out challenging Jesus, *"If you are the Son of God,* command these stones be made bread." When Jesus was on the cross he was still using the same ploy, *"If you are the Son of God,* come down from the cross." (Read SON OF GOD; SON OF MAN by Fred Gregory)

The purpose of this and the previous chapter was to equip you with your very first step in adding this spiritual weapon to your superhero utility belt; that is believing that it is possible even for you. Believe it, embrace it and then begin your exercise regimen. Just know that Holy Spirit will "set you up."

PROPHETIC UTTERANCES

We are indeed emissaries of Christ on the Earth.

Herein is our love made perfect, that we may have boldness in the Day of Judgment: because as he is, so are we in this world. 1 John 4:17

As we learned earlier, Holy Spirit will use your senses to draw your attention to someone. When a person is first nudged or prompted by Holy Spirit with a gift of ministry, the precursor is usually discernment (discerning good and evil), followed by a word of knowledge, word of wisdom, healings, and miracles or prophesy. The first ploy by Satan to squelch it is to whisper, "It's just your imagination."

If your heart is in the right place, you surely do not want to say something that is not from God. By now, I hope that you understand that with your imagination yielded to Holy Spirit that you can trust it.

Elijah learned this concept, first hand.

And he (The Lord) said, Go forth, and stand upon the mount before the LORD. And, behold, the LORD passed by, and a great and strong wind rent the mountains, and brake in pieces the rocks before the LORD; but the LORD was not in the wind: and after the wind an earthquake; but the LORD was not in the earthquake: And after the earthquake a fire; but the LORD was not in the fire: and after the fire a still small voice.

And it was so, when Elijah heard it, that he wrapped his face in his mantle, and went out, and stood in the entering in of the cave. And, behold, there came a voice unto him, and said, What do thou hear, Elijah? 1Kings 19:11-13

That sounds like the cell phone commercial that keeps asking, "Can you hear me, now." God is asking that same question of each of us. "Son/daughter, can you hear me now?"

YOUR IMAGINATION IS THE INTERFACE BETWEEN YOUR SPIRIT MAN AND THE SPIRIT OF GOD

I hope you have the first spiritual weapon, **exercised senses**, secured to your belt. Now let's look at another weapon of our spiritual warfare that is strong to pulling down those strongholds and casting out those vain imaginations. It is found in Romans Chapter twelve. It too is an ongoing process.

I beseech you therefore, brethren, by the mercies of God, that ye present your bodies a living sacrifice, holy, acceptable unto God, which is your reasonable service. Rom 12:1

And be not conformed to this world: but be ye transformed by the renewing of your mind, that ye may prove what is that good, and acceptable, and perfect, will of God. Rom 12:2

WOW! With the first weapon, we through practice can learn to discern good from evil, and with this one we can prove (That is we can demonstrate) what the good, acceptable, and perfect will of God is. Boy Howdy! That's amazing. This one is also a process. We must present ourselves to God as a living sacrifice; that is to totally yield ourselves to Him. That is a decision of the will. This is so easy to say but so hard to implement. We are told that this is our reasonable service or method of worship—either way it is expected of all of us who call ourselves Christians. So, if it is expected, then it is possible. I like the way a friend of mine, a young minister from Adelaide, Australia, Chris Blackeby expresses it. He says, "I just need to believe what I know."[3] Our part is to just to believe it is ours because Jesus did everything else for us.

Before we investigate our weapons further allow me to clear something up. When we gave our heart to God and believed on Jesus and received Him as savior, we received all that Jesus is. We are the righteousness of God through Christ Jesus. The problem is to believe that with all of its ramifications, benefits, and authority. Those strongholds, vain imaginations and thoughts that try to supersede the Word of God are weapons sent from the enemy to squelch our believing who we are in Christ, and to veil our true identity.

Even though it is an ongoing process, we are shown what must be done to kick it off. We are told not to be conformed to this world system but be transformed by the renewing of our mind. So then, we have to abandon one mind set and totally buy into a new one. As this transformation—this metamorphosis progresses, we should become more and more alien like in our actions, our beliefs, our demeanor, and our countenance when compared to non-Christians who are part of this world system.

This sounds like an unattainable goal. That is one of the ploys of the enemy. This is one of those thoughts that tries to elevate itself above the Word of God. But what is the truth? Just look at what Paul wrote about the purpose of the fivefold ministry. You remember those five mantles that Jesus distributed to His body upon his ascension back to heaven. Look at Ephesians chapter four and verses twelve and thirteen. *For the perfecting of the saints, for the work of the ministry, for the edifying of the body of Christ: Till we all come in the unity of the faith, and of the knowledge of the Son of God, unto a perfect man, unto the measure of the stature of the fulness of* **Christ:** Not only is this attainable but it is expected of each Christian.

Unfortunately, those of us who are Charismatic or Pentecostal have often tended to completely disregard the mind in search of Spiritual Mindedness. Holy Spirit considers the mind important enough to encourage us to have it renewed. We must not throw the baby out with the bath. We will dig a bit deeper into this later.

The Apostle Paul sets the stage in Romans chapter 12 with these two verses and then he proceeds to discuss some of the details of this mind transforming procedure. Beginning in verse three he begins to talk about offices, giftings, practices, or anointings given to individuals by God the Father. Don't confuse these Offices with the Fivefold Ascension Gifts of the Son, nor the Gifts of the Spirit. This list associated with this spiritual weapon reminds me of a Swiss Army Knife. It has a lot of blades and gadgets in one handy weapon.

...God (theos) has dealt (distributed-given out) a measure of faith for we are all members of one body but different offices. [praxis-to practice or function in—like a law practice of medical practice] Rom 12:3

So then to begin this journey and to be able to wield this weapon we must begin identifying and walking in the offices in which our Heavenly Father has endowed us. Remember that we are looking at spiritual weapons that we can use to pull down strongholds and cast down those vain imaginations. The weapons that we have studied thus far can do much more than that; however this is a vital area where they can be used by you and me.

As mighty as the first two weapons of our warfare, the next one is simply amazing. This weapon of our warfare can be found in Ephesians chapter one.

Before we investigate this next weapon, let me make something clear. The Apostle Paul prayed a similar prayer for several of the churches for which he was Apostle. It was very important in his mind, but I am afraid that we have missed the true meaning.

Wherefore I also, after I heard of your faith in the Lord Jesus, and love unto all the saints, Cease not to give thanks for you, making mention of you in my prayers; That the God of our Lord Jesus Christ, the Father of glory, may give unto you the spirit of wisdom and revelation in the knowledge of him: The eyes of your understanding being enlightened; that ye may know what is the hope of his calling, and what the riches of the glory of his inheritance in the saints, And what is the exceeding greatness of his power to us-ward who believe, according to the working of his mighty power, Which he wrought in Christ, when he raised him from the dead, and set him at his own right hand in the heavenly places, Far above all principality, and power, and might, and dominion, and every name that is named, not only in this world, but also in that which is to come: Eph. 1:15-21

We are going to focus our attention on verses seventeen and eighteen.

[Do you agree with me that Holy Spirit does not have a limited vocabulary and that He picked each word that he inspired the writers of the Bible to pen? Look with me at the original language to get insight into what He said]

Eph 1:17 *That the God of our Lord Jesus Christ, the Father of glory, may give unto you the spirit of <u>wisdom</u> and <u>revelation</u> in the <u>knowledge of him:</u>*

(Wisdom) sophia *sof-ee'-ah* wisdom (higher or lower, worldly or spiritual):--wisdom. *(Sophistication—Sophisticated Wisdom)*

(Revelation) apokalupsis *ap-ok-al'-oop-sis* disclosure*:*--appearing, coming, lighten, manifestation, be revealed, revelation.

(Knowledge) epignosis *ep-ig'-no-sis* recognition, i.e. (by implication) *full discernment*, acknowledgement:--(ac-) knowledge(-ing, - ment).

Now put it together and read it.

That the God of our Lord Jesus Christ, the Father of glory, may give unto you the spirit of sophisticated wisdom and disclosure in the full discernment of Him.

Now let's dissect verse eighteen.

The eyes of your understanding being enlightened; that ye may know what is the hope of his calling, and what the riches of the glory of his inheritance in the saints,

(Eyes) ophthalmos *of-thal-mos'* the eye (literally or figuratively); by implication, *vision*; figuratively, envy (from the jealous side-glance):--eye, sight.

(Understanding) dianoia *dee-an'-oy-ah* deep thought, properly, the faculty (mind or its disposition), by implication, its exercise:--*imagination*, mind, understanding

(Enlightened) *fo-tid'-zo* *(Photograph—engulfed in His Light)* to shed rays, i.e. to shine or (transitively) to brighten up (literally or figuratively):--enlighten, illuminate, (bring to, give) light, make to see.

Now read both verses together.

That the God of our Lord Jesus Christ, the Father of glory, may give unto you the spirit of SOPHISTICATED WISDOM AND DISCLOSURE in the FULL DISCERNMENT OF HIM. The VISION of your IMAGINATION being ENGULFED IN HIS LIGHT that you may know what is the hope of his calling and what the riches of the glory of his inheritance in the saints.

The process of having the light of God to engulf the vision of our imagination and to have the full discernment of Jesus disclosed to the saints was so important that the Apostle Paul mentioned it in the introduction to most of his epistles to the churches, such as

*But as it is written, Eye hath not seen, nor ear heard, neither have entered into the heart of man, the things which God hath prepared for them that love him. But God hath revealed them unto us by his Spirit: for the Spirit searches all things, yea, the deep things of God. For what man knows the things of a man, save the spirit of man which is in him? Even so the things of God knows no man, but the Spirit of God. Now we have received, not the spirit of the world, but the spirit which is of God; that we might know the things that are freely given to us of God. Which things also we speak, not in the words which man's wisdom teaches, but which the Holy Spirit teaches; comparing spiritual things with spiritual. But the natural man receives not the things of the Spirit of God: for they are foolishness unto him: neither can he know them, because they are spiritually discerned. But he that is spiritual judges **(discerns)** all things, yet he himself is judged of no man. For who hath known the mind of the Lord, that he may instruct him? But we have the mind of Christ. 1 Cor. 2:9-16*

Jesus' imagination was "perfectly" in line with the Father; therefore He imagined a thing, spoke it and it manifested.

Our goal must be to have our imagination totally yielded to Him and when we speak a thing it will manifest. This comes through the Spirit of DISCLOSURE and the Spirit of SOPHISTICATED WISDOM of the FULL DISCERNMENT OF HIM.

At this juncture, I feel that I must make an important statement. The truths presented here cannot be discovered; they must be revealed by Holy Spirit. With His help I have attempted to guide you toward them and make you hungry for the revelation. Brothers and Sisters, pray this prayer for yourselves continually until *the vision of your imagination is fully engulfed in His light.*

Now we have learned how to use some of the spiritual weapons of warfare available to us through Holy Spirit and are applying them to our lives and especially to our imaginations in the continuing process of casting down the vain imaginations and thoughts that elevate themselves above the knowledge of God. The next time that the enemy whispers, "It's just your imagination," you can answer**,** *"Yes, Devil it is all in my imagination; and my imagination is coming more and more into perfect alignment with the will of God in Christ Jesus!!"*

The preceding precepts are important stones in the foundation that allows us to move into the Mysteries of the Kingdom of God. Armed with the knowledge of who we are; that is disciples of Jesus and having been even better equipped we must now be proactive in digging into scripture and allowing Holy Spirit full access to our imagination to REVEAL to us the *Mysteries of the Kingdom* for this generation.

Take a deep breath. Go for it!

CHAPTER 3

MYSTERIES OF THE KINGDOM OF GOD

PRAYER

It would be foolish indeed to begin a trek like the one ahead of us without first covering ourselves, head-to-toe and inside and out with intense diligent prayer. I suggest that you pray the prayer that we just learned for yourself frequently throughout the journey. It is from Eph 1:17-18.

My prayer for all who take this trip is

That the God of our Lord Jesus Christ, the Father of glory, may give unto you the spirit of *SOPHISTICATED WISDOM AND DISCLOSURE* in the *FULL DISCERNMENT OF HIM.*

And that the *VISION* of your IMAGINATION being ENGULFED IN HIS LIGHT that you may know

What is the hope of his calling [invitation]
What are the riches of the glory of his inheritance in the saints
What is the exceeding great power to us who believes

WARNING

When these mysteries of the Kingdom of God are revealed to your spirit, they will always line up with the written Word of God. {Not necessarily your interpretation of the Word} These mysteries are hidden FOR us in plain sight—in many scriptures that have been so familiar to the Church for years. It would be grossly hypocritical of me to admonish you to test all of your revelations by the Bible and not do so myself herein. Therefore because this is an in depth study it is necessary to present you with many scriptural references. Please do not just scan over them or avoid them altogether. It is within those Holy Spirit inspired writings that these mysteries are hidden. They may be referred to as "TREASURES OF DARKNESS."

And I will give thee the treasures of darkness, and hidden riches of secret places, that thou may know that I, the LORD, which call thee by thy name, am the God of Israel. Isa 45:3

****

A **MYSTERY** is something that is hidden from sight; something that seems to contradict reason or known facts; something that defies logic. A mystery is something that is out of place; an enigma; an anomaly. A Mystery cannot be readily comprehended nor explained. A mystery may be so well hidden that we do not realize that it even exists, even though we are exposed to it—it is hidden in plain sight.

We humans are born with an attraction to that which is mysterious. That is why we often risk everything to explore new lands; new worlds; why we invent new machines and experiment to discover new methods of doing things. Scientific and medical advances are forthcoming because we constantly push away the darkness of mystery to get a glimpse beyond. Many of our classic stories, books, and movies are mysteries written by such authors such as Agatha Christie, Ellery Queen, and Alfred Hitchcock. Many of the games that we indulge in mesmerize us because they challenge our mind to "solve the mystery." Whether it's just a crossword puzzle, a su-do-ku, or Rubik's Cube, we have a need to find the answer. The unraveling of a mystery often challenges the current longstanding accepted truth within any discipline. Einstein's theory of relativity was a fly in the ointment of accepted "truth" about our universe for decades. Einstein himself thought it was "an irritating theory" because it inferred that the universe had to have been created. He even divided by Zero to disprove it. Years later he said that that was the worst mistake of his career.[3]

A *SPIRITUAL MYSTERY* has many of the same attributes and characteristics as a natural mystery with one important caveat: *ultimately Spiritual Mysteries cannot be discovered; they must be revealed.*

Howbeit we speak wisdom among them that are perfect: yet not the wisdom of this world, nor of the princes of this world, that come to naught: But we speak the wisdom of God in a mystery, even the hidden wisdom, which God ordained before the world unto our glory: Which none of the princes of this world knew: for had they known it, they would not have crucified the Lord of glory.

But as it is written, Eye hath not seen, nor ear heard, neither have entered into the heart of man, the things which God hath prepared for them that love him. But God hath revealed them unto us by his Spirit: for the Spirit searches all things, yea, the deep things of God. For what man knows the things of a man, save the spirit of man which is in him? Even so the things of God knows no man, but the Spirit of God. Now we have received, not the spirit of the world, but the spirit which is of God; that we might know the things that are freely given to us of God. Which things also we speak, not in the words which man's wisdom teaches, but which the Holy Spirit teaches; comparing spiritual things with spiritual.

But the natural man receives not the things of the Spirit of God: for they are foolishness unto him: neither can he know them, because they are spiritually discerned.

But he that is spiritual judges all things, yet he himself is judged of no man. For who hath known the mind of the Lord, that he may instruct him? But we have the mind of Christ. 1 Cor.2:6-16

Please pause and take the time to read those eleven verses aloud at least three times while praying the prayer for yourself from Eph 1:17-18.

WOW! Are you beginning to see the mystery hidden in plain sight right here in front of you? Are a whole bunch of other scriptures rushing to your spirit and being lit-up by the revelation from Holy Spirit? It's like a jigsaw puzzle. You have found the one piece that connects several other sections of the picture that you have been working on. Now you can make out Mickey Mouse's face clearly in your puzzle. I told you it was going to be an awesome ride.

If we can collect ourselves after that download, we will proceed.

****

1 CORINTHIANS 2:9-16

We can hinge this whole teaching on this short passage of scripture. We will break it down line by line and precept upon precept and back it up with many other passages.

***One note must be interjected here. We have stated that these spiritual mysteries cannot be discovered but they must be revealed. This revelation is in a special category. There are three categories of divine revelation.

They are:

1. Typical/general revelation—reveals details about God's plans for individuals, fellowships, cities, nations, and the world.
2. Inspiration—special revelation to write the inerrant Word of God—Scripture
3. Mystery Revelation—revelation that reveals mysteries hidden by the Lord for us. LINE UPON LINE

Verse 6

Howbeit we speak wisdom among them that are perfect: yet not the wisdom of this world, nor of the princes of this world, that come to nought:

This is the Apostle Paul writing to the church at Corinth. In verse six he identifies the group that his epistle is meant for—the perfect—the mature Christian just as this book is aimed at that same audience--*you*.

Verse 7

But we speak the wisdom of God in a mystery, even the hidden wisdom, which God ordained before the world unto our glory:

He said that God hid this wisdom before creation—not from us but *for us* for our glory and benefit to be revealed at the appropriate time. Paul is saying that the appropriate time is ***NOW***. This mystery had been revealed to him and he was now going to reveal it to them.

What exactly was that mystery that he was going to reveal to those mature in the Lord? The answer is found in verse eight.

Verse 8

Which none of the princes of this world knew: for had they known it, they would not have crucified the Lord of glory. (Princes of this world—Jesus called Satan the prince of this world-- Of judgment, because the prince of this world is judged.) John 16:11

What would be wrong with that? Wouldn't it have been better that Jesus wasn't crucified? ***No***, because He had to die for the sins of the world; past, present, and future. He had to die to secure your and my salvation. Had the mystery not been hidden from Satan, the Princes of Darkness could have blocked the salvation of the whole world by *not killing* the Messiah. Now we know it was *hidden from them and for us.* So then the mystery that Paul is referring to here is the mystery of the Cross. (This revealed mystery includes more than the events on Calvary that Friday.)

Now to him that is of power to establish you according to my gospel, and the preaching of Jesus Christ, according to the revelation of the mystery, which was kept secret since the world began, But now is made manifest, and by the scriptures of the prophets, according to the commandment of the everlasting God, made known to all nations for the obedience of faith: Rom. 16:25-26

This mystery is now being made known to the world—for all men to have access to God through Jesus.

Having made known unto us the mystery of his will, according to his good pleasure which he hath purposed in himself: That in the dispensation of the fullness of times he might gather together in one all things in Christ, both which are in heaven, and which are on earth; even in him: Eph. 1:9-10

This is the mystery of the Cross: that the Creator became the Created and suffered death to pay for the sins of the world.

OTHER MYSTERIES REVEALED

The Mystery of Gentiles As Fellow Heirs of Salvation

I say then, Have they stumbled that they should fall? God forbid: but rather through their fall salvation is come unto the Gentiles, for to provoke them to jealousy. Rom. 11:11

If ye have heard of the dispensation of the grace of God which is given me to you-ward: How that by revelation he made known unto me the mystery; (as I wrote afore in few words, Whereby, when ye read, ye may understand my knowledge in the mystery of Christ) Which in other ages was not made known unto the sons of men, as it is now revealed unto his holy apostles and prophets by the Spirit; That the Gentiles should be fellow heirs, and of the same body, and partakers of his promise in Christ by the gospel: Eph.3:2-6

Even the mystery which hath been hid from ages and from generations, but now is made manifest to his saints: To whom God would make known what is the riches of the glory of this mystery among the Gentiles; which is Christ in you, the hope of glory: Col. 1:26-27

This mystery was hidden from other ages even though it was prophesied. The fullness of time didn't come for this mystery to be revealed until after Jesus was resurrected from the dead.

All these things spoke Jesus unto the multitude in parables; and without a parable spoke he not unto them: That it might be fulfilled which was spoken by the prophet, saying, I will open my mouth in parables; I will utter things which have been kept secret from the foundation of the world. Matt. 13:34-35

And he said unto them, He that hath ears to hear, let him hear. And when he was alone, they that were about him with the twelve asked of him the parable. And he said unto them, Unto you it is given to know the mystery of the kingdom of God: but unto them that are without, all these things are done in parables: That seeing they may see, and not perceive; and hearing they may hear, and not understand; lest at any time they should be converted, and their sins should be forgiven them. Mark 4:9-12

But he answered and said, I am not sent but unto the lost sheep of the house of Israel. Matt. 15:24

The Mystery of The Trinity of God

That their hearts might be comforted, being knit together in love, and unto all riches of the full assurance of understanding, to the acknowledgement of the mystery of God, and of the Father, and of Christ; In whom are hid all the treasures of wisdom and knowledge. Col. 2:2-3

For in him dwells all the fullness of the Godhead bodily. Col. 2:9

The Mystery of The Body of Christ—The Church

*For we are members of his body, of his flesh, and of his bones. For this cause shall a man leave his father and mother, and shall be joined unto his wife, and they two shall be one flesh. This is a **great mystery**: but I speak concerning Christ and the church.* Eph. 5:30-32

The Mystery of Faith & Godliness as attributes of a Deacon

*Holding the **mystery of the faith** in a pure conscience.*

*And without controversy great is the **mystery of godliness:** God was manifest in the flesh, justified in the Spirit, seen of angels, preached unto the Gentiles, believed on in the world, received up into glory.* 1Tim. 3:9 & 16

The Mystery of The Rapture

Behold, I show you a mystery; We shall not all sleep, but we shall all be changed, In a moment, in the twinkling of an eye, at the last trump: for the trumpet shall sound, and the dead shall be raised incorruptible, and we shall be changed. 1 Cor. 15:51-52

But I would not have you to be ignorant, brethren, concerning them which are asleep, that ye sorrow not, even as others which have no hope. For if we believe that Jesus died and rose again, even so them also which sleep in Jesus will God bring with him. For this we say unto you by the word of the Lord, that we which are alive and remain unto the coming of the Lord shall not prevent them which are asleep. For the Lord himself shall descend from heaven with a shout, with the voice of the archangel, and with the trump of God: and the dead in Christ shall rise first: Then we which are alive and remain shall be caught up together with them in the clouds, to meet the Lord in the air: and so shall we ever be with the Lord. Wherefore comfort one another with these words. 1 Thess. 4:13-18

These are two of the scriptures that describe what the church calls The Rapture, though that word never appears in scripture. Paul refers to it as a mystery—it had never before been revealed to man.

The Mystery of The Blindness of Israel

He came unto his own, and his own received him not. But as many as received him, to them gave he power to become the sons of God, even to them that believe on his name: John 1:11-12

For I would not, brethren, that ye should be ignorant of this mystery, lest ye should be wise in your own conceits; that blindness in part is happened to Israel, until the fullness of the Gentiles be come in. And so all Israel shall be saved: as it is written, There shall come out of Sion the Deliverer, and shall turn away ungodliness from Jacob:

I say then, Have they stumbled that they should fall? God forbid: but rather through their fall salvation is come unto the Gentiles, for to provoke them to jealousy. Rom. 11:25-26 & 11

The Mystery of Lawlessness

Now we beseech you, brethren, by the coming of our Lord Jesus Christ, and by our gathering together unto him, That ye be not soon shaken in mind, or be troubled, neither by spirit, nor by word, nor by letter as from us, as that the day of Christ is at hand. Let no man deceive you by any means: for that day shall not come, except there come a falling away first, and that man of sin be revealed, the son of perdition; Who opposes and exalts himself above all that is called God, or that is worshipped; so that he as God sits in the temple of God, showing himself that he is God. Remember ye not, that, when I was yet with you, I told you these things? And now ye know what withholds that he might be revealed in his time. For the mystery of iniquity doth already work: only he who now lets will let, until he be taken out of the way. And then shall that Wicked be revealed, whom the Lord shall consume with the spirit of his mouth, and shall destroy with the brightness of his coming: Even him, whose coming is after the working of Satan with all power and signs and lying wonders, And with all deceivableness of unrighteousness in them that perish; because they received not the love of the truth, that they might be saved. 2 Thess. 2:1-10

The Mystery of iniquity or lawlessness is a rather large study in itself; far beyond the scope of our current study. Having said that allow me to make a couple of points as briefly as possible. First of all the early 1600's English is hard to understand with today's vernacular. Let's sort through some old English words and phrases. There was a false teaching in the Corinthian Church that the return of Jesus was imminent. Paul says that a couple of events have to occur prior to Jesus' return. First there must come a *falling away* and second that the *man of sin be revealed* as the son of perdition—the one who will exalt himself above God so as to be worshipped as God. The phrase "falling away" is the Greek word apostasia which means to forsake or fall away. Its root comes from the word that means writ of divorcement. This is not referring to a person who is reluctant to receive Jesus as Lord, but one who publicly denounces Jesus. The next phrase to consider is **son** *of perdition.* The Greek word for perdition really means damnable, waste, or destruction. The phrase son of perdition was used by Jesus in John Chapter seventeen.

While I was with them in the world, I kept them in thy name: those that thou gave me I have kept, and none of them is lost, but the son of perdition; that the scripture might be fulfilled. John 17:12

Jesus of course was speaking of Judas. Paul is speaking of the *Antichrist* who is yet to come.

In verse six Paul reminds them that they know who withholds *katecho* hold down (fast), in various applications (literally or figuratively):--have, hold (fast), keep (in memory), let, X make toward, possess, retain, seize on, stay, take, withhold. He is saying that they knew *who was controlling* the situation until the proper time for Antichrist to be revealed. He goes on to say that the *Mystery of Lawlessness* is already at work. This applies even more strongly to the generation that you and I live in. Lawlessness is rampant worldwide. He reiterates that someone is restraining/letting lawlessness until that one who restrains is taken out of the way, and then the Wicked One will be revealed and unrestrained. Paul says, "You just think it's bad now, just you wait; you ain't seen nuttin yet!" I'm sure that it is as clear as mud now, huh?

Okay, okay! I won't leave you hanging. He that is now restraining lawlessness is Holy Spirit. Restraining lawlessness is one of the many *ministries that Holy Spirit does through the Body of Christ.* When the Church is taken away in what we call The Rapture, that particular ministry of Holy Spirit will cease. Then Antichrist will be revealed; lawlessness will be unrestrained and literally "all Hell will break loose" upon the earth. This period is referred to by several names, one is The Great Tribulation. In the twenty-fourth chapter of Matthew, Jesus says that unless those days are shortened that mankind would completely annihilate himself. Such is the Mystery of Lawlessness.

How Mysteries Were Revealed to Apostle Paul

In the twelfth chapter of 2 Corinthians, Paul tries to describe the event wherein he received the revelation concerning these mysteries.

I knew a man in Christ above fourteen years ago, (whether in the body, I cannot tell; or whether out of the body, I cannot tell: God knows ;) such an one caught up to the third heaven. And I knew such a man, (whether in the body, or out of the body, I cannot tell: God knows;) How that he was caught up into paradise, and heard unspeakable words, which it is not lawful for a man to utter. 2 Cor. 12:2-4

I suggest to you that those unspeakable words that were not permitted to be spoken were in fact additional mysteries whose time had not yet come. I believe that the time has finally arrived for many of them to be released.

There were other mysteries that were not allowed to be released in the first century; in addition to the ones that Apostle Paul was shown. I am referring to the mysteries spoken to John in Revelation Chapter ten.

And I saw another mighty angel come down from heaven, clothed with a cloud: and a rainbow was upon his head, and his face was as it were the sun, and his feet as pillars of fire: And he had in his hand a little book open: and he set his right foot upon the sea, and his left foot on the earth, And cried with a loud voice, as when a lion roars: and when he had cried, seven thunders uttered their voices. And when the seven thunders had uttered their voices, I was about to write: and I heard a voice from heaven saying unto me, Seal up those things which the seven thunders uttered, and write them not. Rev. 10:1-4

Both Paul and John were shown mysteries whose time had not come when they were writing and preaching the gospel of the Kingdom of God. The time of the revealing of many has finally arrived.

And the angel which I saw stand upon the sea and upon the earth lifted up his hand to heaven, And swore by him that lives forever and ever, who created heaven, and the things that therein are, and the earth, and the things that therein are, and the sea, and the things which are therein, that there should be time no longer: {No more delay} *But in the days of the voice of the seventh angel, when he shall begin to sound, the mystery of God should be finished, as he hath declared to his servants the prophets.* Rev. 10:5-7

Surely the Lord GOD will do nothing, but he reveals his secret unto his servants the prophets. Amos 3:7

My dear brothers and sisters do not be dismayed or anxious about what you see in the world around you. These mysteries that are yet to be revealed are **hidden for us and from the enemy**. Listen to the prophets of God. Remember it is a partnership. We have dominion of this world and we must occupy and exercise that authority until Jesus returns.

Holy Spirit is releasing strategizes for the Body of Christ to carry out so as to be in position to receive further orders. Unity must come to the Body. We have territorial responsibilities that will be revealed soon.

****

Signs and Wonders

Before we begin the transition from mysteries of the first century generation to the mysteries being revealed to this generation, we have one more avenue to explore.

From our vantage point more than 2,000 years removed from that era, it is a bit hard for us to fathom the affront to conventional thinking and religious tradition that all of these revealed mysteries must have spawned. Israel as a nation rejected the Messiah even though she had anticipated His coming for centuries.

All of those mysteries that were revealed during that era are so much a part of our common understanding of Christianity today that it's tough for us to picture a time when they were radical in-your-face ideas that carried the death penalty when proclaimed or at least imprisonment. Saul of Tarsus was the go-to-guy to put a stop to such insurrection.

The revealing of all of these mysteries would have been hard enough to swallow under normal circumstances. The first century A.D. was anything but normal. Rome had conquered most of the known world. Israel was once again a besieged nation. The religious leadership had become corrupt trying to compromise with the Roman occupiers in an attempt to maintain their authority with the Jewish people. For them, it was a horrible time for someone to upset the apple cart with seemingly rebellious ideas.

Signs and wonders were part and partial of the Kingdom of God that Jesus brought with Him. They were very practical in validating the preachers of those new revelations—those mysteries. When Jesus was asked by John the Baptist's followers if He was the one or if they should look for another, He told them to report the signs and wonders that He performed as proof. Those powers and abilities were passed on to the Disciples and to us for our own validation as we go into all the world making disciples of all nations.

In this generation Christians are challenged to carry the gospel of the Kingdom to a world that is religious to the nth degree. The followers of many of those religions are adamantly opposed to Christianity as well as Judaism. In the case of Islam, the total annihilation of all Jews and all Christians is taught in many of their schools and Mosques. There are millions of devotees to the Islamic faith. They have had a closed Theistic society governed by the laws of their spiritual leaders for thousands of years. Presenting the gospel of the Kingdom to these people using natural wisdom will have little positive impact. In this generation, signs and wonders must, once again be the hallmark of the Christian Evangelist and laity alike.

CHAPTER 4

THE TRANSITION

Thus far in our quest for the revelation of the mysteries of God—the Treasures of Darkness, we have established a few precepts from scripture. Let's review them before proceeding.

- God had a well conceived plan from before creation
- God hid, in plain sight within His Word many mysteries for our benefit
- God hid these nuggets from the demonic princes of this world
- These mysteries are time sensitive—God reveals them at just the right time
- Many mysteries were revealed through Jesus' ministry
- Many mysteries were revealed at the launching of His Church
- Many Mysteries of God cannot be taught or discovered
- Many Mysteries of God must be revealed

We now have a solid foundation concerning mysteries of God. If we stopped here, we would indeed have a much better understanding of the mysteries of God that were revealed in times past. Already it has helped us better understand concepts and scriptures that were once vague. Your jigsaw puzzle of Mickey Mouse has some large areas filled in. However, there are still many pieces of the puzzle that have not found a home yet.

Our quest is to push on to the mysteries that are presently being revealed and those that are yet to be revealed. Both the scriptures below imply that there are additional mysteries that are being revealed through prophets on a continual basis.

And though I have the gift of prophecy, and understand all mysteries, and all knowledge; and though I have all faith, so that I could remove mountains, and have not charity, I am nothing. 1 Cor. 13:2

For he that speaks in an unknown tongue speaks not unto men, but unto God: for no man understands him; howbeit in the spirit he speaks mysteries.1 Cor. 14:2

One of the offices of the FIVEFOLD MINISTRY given by Jesus after his ascension back to heaven is that of the Prophet. It is obvious then that there are mysteries yet to be revealed. I believe that the fullness of time has come and that they are beginning to be revealed to the Body of Christ.

While it is true that the mysteries of God cannot be discovered, but must be revealed, it is equally true that we can so position ourselves with Jesus that we become a prime candidate for that special revelation.

It is the glory of God to conceal a thing: but the honor of kings is to search out a matter. Prov. 25:2

[For an in depth study of this matter, acquire a copy of the CD series by Bill Johnson of Bethel Church of Redding, Ca called "The Supernatural Power of a Transformed Mind."][1]

As I prayerfully pondered how to convey to you that in which Holy Spirit is enlightening me concerning this matter set before us, He gave me a vision and an analogy that I now relate to you.

Most of us have seen science fiction movies about space exploration. Often there is a scene where a character, encased in his space suit must propel himself from one space ship to another without a lifeline. In the weightlessness of space it does not take a lot of effort to jump the several yards separating the two ships. A fellow astronaut is positioned on the second ship with outstretched hand to grab his friend as he comes near.

Our hero springs and we watch with bated breath as he ever so slowly crosses the gulf and approaches his friend. The friend reaches out and grabs his hand and pulls him to safety. We gulp a breath of air once again.

You are the hero who will have to make that leap. The friend on the other ship is Holy Spirit with his hand outstretched to grab you. As your teacher and ship pilot I must get you as close as possible so as to make that leap as short as possible. *That will be your leap of Faith into the grasp of Holy Spirit.*

****

To proceed we will refer back to our "pilot scripture" in 1 Corinthians. We have covered verses six through eight. Now we will continue with verse nine.

But as it is written, Eye hath not seen, nor ear heard, neither have entered into the heart of man, the things which God hath prepared for them that love him. But God hath revealed them unto us by his Spirit: for the Spirit searches all things, yea, the deep things of God. For what man knows the things of a man, save the spirit of man which is in him? Even so the things of God knows no man, but the Spirit of God.

Now we have received, not the spirit of the world, but the spirit which is of God; that we might know the things that are freely given to us of God. Which things also we speak, not in the words which man's wisdom teaches, but which the Holy Ghost teaches; comparing spiritual things with spiritual.

But the natural man receives not the things of the Spirit of God: for they are foolishness unto him: neither can he know them, because they are spiritually discerned.

But he that is spiritual judges all things, yet he himself is judged of no man. For who hath known the mind of the Lord, that he may instruct him? But we have the mind of Christ. 1 Cor. 2:9-16

Verse 9

But as it is written, Eye hath not seen, nor ear heard, neither have entered into the heart of man, the things which God hath prepared for them that love him.

Here we are told that the mysteries hidden in God for us are not discoverable, and that we as well as the demonic forces are totally oblivious to their very existence. Not only have we not seen or heard but we haven't even entertained their possibility in our wildest (unsanctified) imaginations.

This is not referring *ONLY* to the 'sweet bye-n-bye' in Heaven, but also upon this earth. So then there is no earthly way for a human being to be able to even broach these mysteries much less plumb their depths. We don't even know they exist. There is a stanza from an old Ogden Nash poem "I will arise and go now," that sums it up pretty well.

> *Indeed, the*
> *Ignorant Have-Not*
> *Don't even know*
> *What he don't got.*[2]

Some poor souls have touted, "Ignorance is Bliss." With a great sigh of resignation they proclaim, "Some things are just not for us (as Christians) to know. The Lord moves in mysterious ways, His word to perform. We just shouldn't question some things." I have a word for that kind of 'stinkin thinkin.' That word is BOLOGNY. Scripture says test all things and hold fast to that which is good.

Present company, as the axiom goes, is of course excluded from that kind of reasoning. The fact that you have made it this far indicates that you are not of that ilk. Having said that allow me to throw in a disclaimer. We must never become arrogant because of any revelation or understanding from Holy Spirit. God forbid. Freely we receive and freely we must give to those who will receive. As we continue this journey while praying that the vision of our imagination be engulfed in the light of Jesus, we must also pray the same prayer for those who are *not ready* to receive yet. There will still be those of the Body of Christ who will resist enlightenment with all of their strength, because with revelation knowledge comes accountability.

Those folks just described stop with the reading or quoting of verse nine and never go on to verse ten. Since becoming a Christian in 1962 I have heard verse nine quoted at least ten times more often than verse ten. Verse ten has a load of accountability with it.

Verse 10

But God hath revealed them unto us by his Spirit: for the Spirit searches all things, yea, the deep things of God.

Beginning with verse ten and going through verse sixteen you are going to come face-to-face with one of those *Mysteries of God hidden in plain sight.* Please take some time to pray our prayer from Ephesians chapter one and read those verses several times before we go on. We'll wait on you.

Holy Spirit please engulf the vision of our imaginations with the brilliant light of Jesus concerning this mystery. In Jesus' name I pray. Amen

Verse ten begins with a big *BUT.* But God has revealed them unto us by his Spirit. This is part of the fulfillment of Jesus' promise in John chapter sixteen.

I have yet many things to say unto you, but ye cannot bear them now. Howbeit when he, the Spirit of truth, is come, he will guide you into all truth: for he shall not speak of himself; but whatsoever he shall hear, that shall he speak: and he will show you things to come. John 16:12-13

Holy Spirit through the pen of Paul is telling us that although we cannot even detect that there are any nuggets of understanding or paradigm changing mysteries hidden anywhere, by our natural abilities, that we are not limited to those abilities. He is saying that we have access to those gems by the Holy Spirit in communication with our regenerated spirit via our imagination. WOW!

Forever, the anointed teacher, Paul in the last part of verse ten begins his explanation of how this truly amazing proclamation is true. He says that Holy Spirit who is God searches everything about God and knows the infinite depths of God. Chew on that one for a minute. Next he draws a comparison between the Spirit of God and the spirit of man so that we can get a better handle on what he has just said before building on it.

Take another deep breath while I put this approach into perspective for you. There are three approaches that Holy Spirit uses to communicate Spiritual concepts to our regenerated spirits. I will list them from the basic to the complex.

- Comparing Spiritual to Natural   Parables
  (Basic principles)
- Comparing Spiritual to spirit of man   Spiritual Logic
  (Revelatory Concepts)
- Comparing Spiritual to Spiritual
  (No Natural Illustration Exists)

Verse 11

For what man knows the things of a man, save the spirit of man which is in him? Even so the things of God knows no man, but the Spirit of God.

Because he is addressing those who are perfect—mature in Christ, he skips the comparison to natural things and begins with comparing Spiritual to human spirit, since they should have a pretty good working knowledge of their spirit man by now. He says that no one knows the complexities of another person; a man's own spirit is the only one who knows the depths and complexities of that man. A man is his spirit—he cannot be subdivided he is ONE.

On top of that precept he adds that likewise no one knows the things—the mysteries—the plans of God except the Spirit of God. *The Spirit of God is God.* God cannot be subdivided from Holy Spirit. *God He is ONE.* Holy Spirit is God. The only way that we can begin to understand the Trinity of God is to understand that we as humans created in His image are also a Trinity—we are spirit, we have a soul, and we live in a body.

Verse 12

Now we have received, not the spirit of the world, but the spirit which is of God; that we might know the things that are freely given to us of God.

This concept linked with the next two are profound, hidden nuggets but can be brushed aside if we are not careful because they are *hidden in plain sight.*

First, he says we have received that which was freely given—that is none other than the person of God, Holy Spirit Himself as a part of who we are. The God of Creation makes his home within us. Folks, we must never take that for granted. That is truly a mystery of mysteries. Christ in us the hope of glory. WOW!

Not only that, but we have NOT received the spirit of the world. That is we do not have the spirit of the Kingdom of Darkness making his abode in us.

Second, he defines the purpose for Holy Spirit making His home within you and me. It is so *"...that we might know the things that are freely given to us of God."* Please do not miss this. Among those things freely given to us by our Lord is the paradigm shifting *special mystery revelation.* It takes my breath away just to bask in the rhema word that Holy Spirit is bringing forth to my spirit from these words.

Go ahead, close your eyes, allow the splendor of who Jesus is to engulf the vision of your imagination and soar with Holy Spirit far above this world. Soak in the presence of the Lord Jesus. Ask for nothing but to be with Him.

If we all have our feet back on Planet Earth, we'll move forward. Holy Spirit isn't through with this revelation yet. Just hold on!

Verse 13

Which things also we speak, not in the words which man's wisdom teaches, but which the Holy Spirit teaches; comparing spiritual things with spiritual.

Paul says I am already revealing to you these same things. They are these mysteries that God hid from Creation for our benefit to be revealed at this time in human history. He says I'm not teaching human wisdom, of which I have much by way of education and understanding, but what I am teaching is from Holy Spirit Himself and it is on a level infinitely higher than the very best of human reasoning and understanding. This teaching is achieved by comparing *Spiritual with Spiritual.* As great an anointed teacher as Paul was; even he could not teach these Mysteries. He could only take the people so far then revelation directly from God had to take them *and us* the rest of the way.

[Comparing Spiritual with Spiritual is our goal with this study. Nay, it is our destiny. We shall not fail that rendezvous.]

Let's finish piloting our spaceship toward our destination with the last few verses then we will return to verse thirteen to begin our space walk.

*** *By the way the analogy of the spaceship and space walk that I am using is a good example of "comparing the spiritual to the natural."*

Verse 14

But the natural man receives not the things of the Spirit of God: for they are foolishness unto him: neither can he know them, because they are spiritually discerned.

Paul reiterates that the natural man cannot receive or know these mysteries because they are spiritually discerned. Revisit the part of our prayer that we are praying for ourselves along this journey found in Eph 1:17.

That the God of our Lord Jesus Christ, the Father of glory, may give unto you the spirit of *SOPHISTICATED WISDOM AND DISCLOSURE* in the *FULL DISCERNMENT OF HIM*.

Finally, at last we get it. Now we know why Paul prayed this prayer for the churches that he visited.

If a bell just rung for you, a buzzer just sounded or lightening flashed into your understanding, you are well on the way to receiving special mystery revealing revelation. In Eph 1:18 the prayer continues "That the Vision of your imagination be engulfed with His light. The word translated light here is where we get the English word photograph. That happens often to believers. This happens to me regularly. The revelation comes like a 'snapshot' in my imagination. That may have happened to you rather than a bell or a buzzer. If Holy Spirit communicates with you that way, embrace it. *{This is part of the Seer gifting.}*

Verse 15

But he that is spiritual judges all things, yet he himself is judged of no man.

The word translated judges and judged are the same word that is translated ***discern*** in verse 14. A better rendering of verse fifteen would be "But he that is spiritual discerns everything but he himself isn't discerned by anyone." Anyone is referring to someone who is naturally minded. They do not have the spiritual ability of discernment.

Verse 16

For who hath known the mind of the Lord, that he may instruct him? But we have the mind of Christ.

Paul is drawing a contrast between those of us who have Christ in us by His Spirit and those who are natural minded. The renewing of the mind is a process. As we become more spiritual minded, we become less natural minded. Paul is doing two things. One, he is promoting the concept of the Trinity and the fact that the Fullness of the Godhead is in Jesus and that we have the attitude, abilities, imagination—mind of Christ in us. We must strive to manifest that fact in every facet of our lives including revelation.

CHAPTER 5

APPLICATION

As promised we will now revisit 1 Cor. 2:13.

Which things also we speak, not in the words which man's wisdom teaches, but which the Holy Ghost teaches; comparing spiritual things with spiritual.

Questions

Is this just one of those complex philosophical academic exercises that doesn't have any application in the real world, or is it a vastly important world changing communication with God?

If comparing spiritual things with spiritual things is the highest level of teaching that Holy Spirit uses, exactly what is it anyway?

Can I tap into it and if I can, how?

If I manage somehow to position myself so that Holy Spirit teaches me in this manner, what does that look like?

Are there practical applications and if so what are they?

We have discovered that these Mysteries were hidden from Creation *for us* and *hidden from* the princes of this world. We also learned that when a person prays in an unknown/unlearned language—a tongue of angels that he speaks mysteries. With those two concepts in mind let's take a quick look at an extremely important form of secured communication that Holy Spirit uses to thwart the plots and schemes of the evil one.

SECURE COMMUNICATIONS

Several years ago Holy Spirit revealed a concept to me that I had never heard before or since. I now share it with you. So be sure to test it by scripture to see if it is valid. This is certainly one to the spiritual weapons at our disposal as Sons of God. The lord dropped this into my Spirit several years ago. We are engaged in warfare with the forces of darkness and spiritual wickedness in high places. With any army, secure communications are vital. We do not want the enemy to know our plans. Pearl Harbor was a good example of that concept. We were caught by surprise.

When I was in the Air Force, my job was in communications. I had a TOP SECRET/CRYPTO ACCESS security clearance. Of course, the cryptographic equipment that we had back in the '60's is antiquated today. This was during the Vietnam War. I was stationed at Bergstrome AFB, Texas, about 40 miles from President Johnson's ranch, so Air Force One landed there often. Timing is important in military communications. That which is Top Secret today may be in the newspaper tomorrow—after the fact.

One of the "Off Line" Crypto machines that I used was called a KL-7. It used a bank of 6 or 8 rotary disks joined together. These were chosen from a total of about 15 disks. Each disk had numbers all around the edge. Each day we received a coded message telling us which disks to use that day, what order to place them in and which number to set each disk on. When put them into the KL-7 they rotated as a message was typed. It printed the encrypted message on ¼" sticky tape. It printed a series of five letters, a space, five more letters, and a space for the entire message. There was no feel for how long each word really was. This sticky tape was then taped onto a sheet of paper and typed onto a perforated paper tape or onto IBM cards. This was extremely difficult to type because they were not really words or sentences.

If that were not enough, we then ran the second tape through an online Cryptographic unit that electronically encoded the already encoded message. At the receiving end a message would be printed out that was this same series of five letters and a space. The operator there had to type that into his KL-7 using the same arrangement of disks and settings as the sender had used.

Only the most sensitive messages were double encrypted by this method. With my Top Secret/Crypto Access security clearance, I was allowed to set up the KL-7 with the proper keying arrangement for the day, however; one had to have the "need to know" to be allowed to encode or decode any of those messages. Only the shift leader had that authority.

Some of those messages were classified higher than Top Secret. They were classified *"Top Drawer."* {Presidential Authority Only} They were picked up by armed curriers in sealed packages and taken to President Lyndon Johnson at his ranch in Johnson City, Texas.

Another example of secure communications took place during World War II. The United States used members of Navajo tribe of Indians to communicate via radio in their native dialect. They were called "Wind Talkers," or "Code Talkers." The following is an excerpt from Major Howard M. Conner's book THE NAVAJO CODE TALKERS.

CODE TALKERS

Were it not for the Navajos, the Marines would never have taken Iwo Jima!

Major Howard M. Conner
The Navajo <u>Code Talkers</u>

The United States was in serious trouble. Following its disastrous surprise attack on Pearl Harbor, Japan held the <u>upper hand</u> in the Pacific.

Japanese soldiers, wearing the rings of American colleges and high schools, could speak English fluently. Educated in the U.S. these men routinely intercepted, and decoded, American military messages. The U.S. needed what has always eluded a country at war: an unbreakable code.

In February of 1942, <u>Philip Johnston</u>, a civilian engineer and World War I veteran, had an idea. What if America's military forces were to use the Navajo language as the basis of a secret code?

Johnston knew something about that language. The <u>son</u> of Protestant missionaries to the Navajo people, he had spent most of his life on, or <u>near</u>, the reservation. He was one of about 30 non-Navajos who could speak the unwritten, extremely difficult language.

Writing a letter outlining his thoughts, Johnston set in motion a life-changing event for 29 Navajo men living on their ancestral homelands. Within months, those men would use their language to develop a code that was *<u>never broken</u>* during the war.

It remained a national secret until 1968.

When the first Code Talkers were sent into combat, at Guadalcanal, how were they received? The Americans thought they were listening to a Japanese exchange:

I called the 7th Marines and before we finished talking, the radio was buzzing, the telephone was ringing, and then runners came to say that the Japs were talking on our frequency and that they had taken over everything...[1]

When the officer- in-charge figured out it was the Navajos speaking to each other, he gave them a chance to compete against another code breaker. Aaseng continues the story:

Then the colonel had an idea. He said he would keep us on one condition: that I could out-race his "white code" - a cylinder-thing that you sent a coded message on and send by radio...tick, tick, tick. Then the receiver signals he has received the message and gives the roger on it. We both sent messages - with the white cylinder and by voice. Both of us received answers. The race was to see who could decode his answer first. He said, "Are you ready?" I said, "I've started already." "How long will it take you?" I was asked. "Two hours?" "Two hours?! I can get ready in two minutes...and give you a head start," I answered.[2]

How long did it actually take for this new Code Talker to accurately <u>receive</u> and translate his message?

I got the "Roger" on my return message from four units in about four and a half minutes. The other guy was still decoding when I said, "Colonel, when are you going to give up that signal outfit? The Navajos are more efficient."[3]

When we pray with our understanding, guess who is always listening in? That's right, Ole Slewfoot and his minions—the enemies of God and of his people. When we are praying in the Spirit, he doesn't have a clue what plans Holy Spirit is making. No wonder he has tried for over 2,000 years to squelch this ability in God's Army.

Hummm! It seems that God is continually hiding His plans from the enemy and revealing them to us on a "need to know" basis. Our God sure is smart.

Verse 20 of the book of Jude says,

But ye, beloved, building up yourselves on your most holy faith, praying in the Holy Ghost,

****

As we close in on the other spaceship, we must slow down and maneuver carefully. As we slow down, mysteries will be revealed that have been vital since Jesus was born, are vital now, and will be vital in the future.

Like those of us pursuing this study, the disciples of Jesus in John chapter sixteen were going through a transition from following Him by sight to being led by Holy Spirit. If you will forgive me the analogy; Jesus is bringing their spaceship as close as possible before they have to make the leap.

These things have I spoken unto you in proverbs: but the time will come, when I shall no more speak unto you in proverbs, but I shall show you plainly of the Father.

At that day ye shall ask in my name: and I say not unto you, that I will pray the Father for you: For the Father himself loves you, because ye have loved me, and have believed that I came out from God.

> *I came forth from the Father, and am come into the world: again, I leave the world, and go to the Father.*
>
> *His disciples said unto him, Lo, now speak thou plainly, and speak no proverb. Now are we sure that thou know all things, and need not that any man should ask thee: by this we believe that thou came forth from God.*
>
> *Jesus answered them, "Do ye now believe?"* John 16:25-31

In this passage from John's writings, Jesus is telling the twelve disciples that He has up to this point taught them in parables but that the day would come when He would show them plainly. He was referring to the time when they could compare spiritual with spiritual.

In verse 29 they jumped the gun and thought they had nailed it. They declared that now that He spoke plainly they understood that he came from God. They were probably pretty proud of themselves. Jesus had not said anything differently than what He had told them time and time again; that He came from the Father and that He was returning to Him. His next statement to them is the clincher that reveals that they still didn't git-it.

> *Behold the hour cometh, yea, is now come, that ye shall be scattered, every man to his own, and shall leave me alone: and yet I am not alone, because the Father is with me.* John 16:32

There are two reasons that Jesus knew that the disciples were not enlightened to what He was saying. First of all, He discerned it in their spirits. Secondly He knew that He was talking about comparing the spiritual with the spiritual and that they were not capable of doing that just yet. The Holy Spirit had not come upon them yet, so they were incapable of comparing spiritual with spiritual. In chapter twenty, John writes

Then said Jesus to them again, Peace be unto you: as my Father hath sent me, even so send I you. And when he had said this, he breathed on them, and said unto them, Receive ye the Holy Spirit: John 20:21-22

You may be struggling with the assertion that I made about our being one with Jesus from verse twelve of chapter fourteen. I really want you to consider it and ponder it as you continue with this teaching. In chapter seventeen, Jesus demonstrates how very important this concept is. This is truly comparing spiritual to spiritual.

Then in the fullness of time when the day of Pentecost came they were all filled with the Holy Spirit. They received the ability to tap into the power of the Holy Spirit and compare spiritual with spiritual. As a result, among all of the signs and wonders that they performed, one of the most important was to reveal never before known mysteries that changed the world.

CHAPTER 6

COMPARING SPIRITUAL TO SPIRITUAL

The following is a rather lengthy portion of scripture however it is vital for your quest to learn how to position yourself to attract *The Mystery Revealing Revelation* of God. Therefore, please read it carefully.

There was a man of the Pharisees, named Nicodemus, a ruler of the Jews: The same came to Jesus by night, and said unto him, "Rabbi, we know that thou art a teacher come from God: for no man can do these miracles that thou doest, except God be with him."

Jesus answered and said unto him, "Verily, verily, I say unto thee, Except a man be born again, he cannot see the kingdom of God."

Nicodemus said unto him, "How can a man be born when he is old? can he enter the second time into his mother's womb, and be born?"

Jesus answered, "Verily, verily, I say unto thee, Except a man be born of water and of the Spirit, he cannot enter into the kingdom of God. That which is born of the flesh is flesh; and that which is born of the Spirit is spirit. Marvel not that I said unto thee, Ye must be born again. The wind blows where it will, and thou hear the sound thereof, but cannot tell where it comes from, and whither it goes: so is every one that is born of the Spirit."

Nicodemus answered and said unto him, "How can these things be?"

Jesus answered and said unto him, "Art thou a master of Israel, and know not these things? Verily, verily, I say unto thee, We speak that we do know, and testify that we have seen; and ye receive not our witness.

If I have told you earthly things, and ye believe not, how shall ye believe, if I tell you of heavenly things?" John 3:1-12

In verse two Nicodemus is saying all of the right words, but he is not sincere about what he is saying. He is a teacher of the Law and a Ruler of the Jews and does not recognize the works of the long awaited Messiah. Instead ole Nic sees this carpenter as a competitor for the attention and respect of the Jews. We know this by the way Jesus addresses him.

Nic never asked a question, yet it seems that in verse three Jesus is answering an unspoken question. Actually Jesus is making a statement based on the attitude of Nicodemus' heart. He says that unless you are born again you can't even see the Kingdom of God. Jesus was manifesting the Kingdom of God from the git-go. He brought the Kingdom—King's dominion—with Him when he arrived on earth. Nicodemus, **seeing** does not perceive the Kingdom—he cannot.

Jesus drops down a few levels and attempts to allow him to *see* the Kingdom by comparing spiritual with natural. He uses the analogy of child birth to convey the basic concept of the spiritual.

{We still use that same analogy after more than 2,000 years to explain what happens in the spirit when we receive Christ's atonement for our sins—we are born again.}

In verse four, ole Nic probably looked like a 'deer in the headlights.' He was completely dumbfounded. He knew that he was totally out of his league with this guy. He probably wished that he had stayed home and watched some rerun on TV Land.

In Verse five and six Jesus repeats the comparison and adds an explanation. He says that which is born of flesh is flesh and that which is born of spirit is spirit. Then in verses seven and eight He tries a little different approach. He compares one who is born of the spirit like the wind that blows. We hear the sound or the manifestation of it but we can't tell where it came from or where it is going.

Nicodemus is still bewildered and more confused than ever. He is like a lost ball in high weeds. He is in way over his head. Jesus scolds him in verse ten because he is a teacher—a master of Israel and cannot comprehend what is being said.

Verse twelve is the clincher. Jesus said, "Nicodemus you don't even understand the earthly comparisons that I have drawn, how in the world could you possibly understand if I tried to tell you of heavenly things—if I compared spiritual things to spiritual?" He is challenging you and me with that same question. That is why all of that swirling is going on in your mind. That is why you always feel that there is spiritual 'things' just out of your reach. You seem to be able to touch them with the finger tips of your spirit, but you can't grasp them. Jesus through His Holy Spirit wants you to be in a place with Him where He can compare spiritual things with spiritual with you.

Wow! You just got a revelation from Holy Spirit that is beginning to tie all of this together, didn't you?

****

My prayer for all who take this trip is

That the God of our Lord Jesus Christ, the Father of glory, may give unto you the spirit of SOPHISTICATED WISDOM AND DISCLOSURE in the FULL DISCERNMENT OF HIM. And that the VISION of your IMAGINATION being ENGULFED IN HIS LIGHT that you may know

What is the hope of his calling [invitation];
What are the riches of the glory of his inheritance in the saints;
What is the exceeding great power to us who believe.

Now allow me to help you put on your *"Faithsuit."* You will need it to make your leap. The faithsuit does not belong to you. You did not bring it on the flight. This faithsuit is furnished by Father God. The material that it is made of is The FAITH OF GOD.

So then faith cometh by hearing, and hearing by the word of God. Rom. 10:17

It says faith comes by *hearing* not *having heard* the word of God. As you read and reread this teaching *you are hearing* the word of God for it is replete with direct scripture references. That is what Holy Spirit will quicken to your spirit and give you the now word—a personal word. The word translated Word here in Romans is *Rhema* the now word—the hearing word—revelation. Holy Spirit is revealing to your spirit that which I cannot convey to you by mere words on a page. EVERY RHEMA ALWAYS COMES WITH SUFFICIENT FAITH TO PERFORM IT.

To restate what my friend Chris Blackeby says, "I JUST HAVE TO BELIEVE WHAT I KNOW."

Heavenly Things

There is a myriad of concepts concerning spiritual things and the Kingdom of God that have natural or earthly counterparts—images—shadows. Jesus taught the masses only by the use of parables. Most still could not even understand the parables. However, those who had 'ears to hear' could understand. Pastors, evangelists, and teachers use this time proven method to convey spiritual truths to the Body of Christ. However, in this generation Holy Spirit desires to take those of us who will answer the invitation to a new level in our spiritual understanding.

I am going to make some bold statements that you must prayerfully consider. For about the last three years Holy Spirit has been continually telling me that He wants to communicate to the Body of Christ, without the use of parables, stories, and analogies. *He wants to communicate raw spiritual precepts; precepts that are not diluted from their purity by these other methods.*

Then a few weeks ago I had the opportunity to listen to the CD series by Bill Johnson, Senior Pastor of Bethel Church in Redding California entitled *"The Supernatural Power of a Transformed Mind."* In that presentation, Pastor Johnson used the third chapter of John to confirm to me what Holy Spirit has been showing me for these three years.

He explained that the Heavenly things that Jesus was referring to with his discussion with Nicodemus were *Heavenly or Spiritual concepts that have no Earthly counterpart.* There simply is no way to compare them. *They must be revealed directly from Holy Spirit to man's spirit via our imagination.*[1]

I am not alone in this nudging from Holy Spirit. This is an outpouring of that same Holy Spirit with mysteries pertinent to *this generation* upon those who have an ear to hear. You have been invited by Lord Jesus to participate in that outpouring.

Is it any wonder then that

YOU <u>MUST</u> KNOW MORE;
YOU HAVE A GREAT GNAWING ON THE INSIDE TO UNDERSTAND;
YOU ETERNALLY CRAVE DEEPER INTIMACY WITH JESUS;
YOUR MIND IS SWIRLING, TRYING TO CATCH UP WITH THE TREMENDOUS OUTPOURING FROM GOD INTO YOUR SPIRIT

Jesus, the Son of Man walked perfectly in this. He is our example. He did not do this as Son of God, but as Son of Man empowered by Holy Spirit; the same Holy Spirit that He sent to us to accomplish the same thing in you and me. WOW!

Now do you understand what Paul was talking about in our 'pilot' scripture?

Which things also we speak, not in the words which man's wisdom teaches, but which the Holy Spirit teaches; comparing spiritual things with spiritual. 1 Cor. 2:13

A good illustration of comparing spiritual things with spiritual can be found at the Lord's last supper. Jesus begins to reveal great MYSTERIES OF THE KINGDOM hidden in plain sight to the disciples and by extension to you and me. Jesus realizes that the most important turning point of all of history was at hand. This dissertation by Jesus needs to be read and reread and playfully pondered by every Christian. We pick it up in the writings of the Apostle John in chapter fourteen, verse one.

Let not your heart be troubled: ye believe in God, believe also in me. In my Father's house are many mansions: if it were not so, I would have told you. I go to prepare a place for you. And if I go and prepare a place for you, I will come again, and receive you unto myself; that where I am, there ye may be also. John 14:1-3

Why did Jesus have to go to prepare a place for us; why wasn't it created when the universe was created? Could it be that only the resurrected SON-OF-MAN had the authority to prepare it? See my book *Son of God; Son of Man*

And whither I go ye know, and the way ye know.

Thomas saith unto him, Lord, we know not whither thou goest; and how can we know the way? John 14:4-5

Thomas put voice to what the others were thinking—"We don't even know where you are going, Lord so how in the world could we know how to get there?" They were probably thinking that if He was going to Jericho, Damascus, or some other far away city that they would know the route to take. Jesus' answer baffled them even more,

Jesus saith unto him, I am the way, the truth, and the life: no man cometh unto the Father, but by me. If ye had known me, ye should have known my Father also: and from henceforth ye know him, and have seen him. John 14:6-7

Jesus' answer was comparing spiritual with spiritual. The twelve disciples do not get it. We can deduce this by the next statement that is made. This time it comes from Philip.

Philip saith unto him, Lord, shew us the Father, and it sufficeth us.

Jesus saith unto him, Have I been so long time with you, and yet hast thou not known me, Philip? he that hath seen me hath seen the Father; and how sayest thou then, Shew us the Father? Believest thou not that I am in the Father, and the Father in me? the words that I speak unto you I speak not of myself: but the Father that dwelleth in me, he doeth the works. Believe me that I am in the

Father, and the Father in me: or else believe me for the very works' sake. John 14:8-11

Jesus is saying that Father God and He are one. In the Jewish culture and religion this was blasphemy; to equate oneself with God. It was hard enough to consider Jesus to be The Son of God, but now He is going even further and claiming divinity for Himself. This undoubtedly produced internal turmoil in the heart of each man, and was debated between each other. They were not YET equipped to understand raw spiritual concepts. Jesus, realizing their confusion, gave them an out. He admonished them that if they could not understand and believe what He had just told them, that they could believe that He was sent from God because of all of the miracles that they had witnessed. I don't know about you, but I know that in my own life, Jesus has allowed me to understand spiritual ideas (dimly) through natural examples when I have been unable to receive the purely spiritual concepts.

Holy Spirit, as my teacher, I thank you for your help in that respect, but my prayer is that "I will never be satisfied with that, but ever open myself up that I may be able to receive more and more of the pure rhema of your teachings—MYSTERIES OF THE KINGDOM HIDDEN IN PLAIN SIGHT."

If what He has just said wasn't mind blowing enough, Jesus adds a prophecy to these sayings in verse twelve. He has just let them off the hook a bit by saying that they should believe that He and the Father are one because of the works that He has done, now he says that if they believe in Him that they will be doing even greater works than He did. WOW!

Verily, verily, I say unto you, He that believeth on me, the works that I do shall he do also; and greater works than these shall he do; because I go unto my Father. John 14:12

Jesus has just proclaimed that the proof that He is one with the Father is the miracles that He did, then if they (and we) do even greater works it implies that miracles would be proof that they (and we) would be one with Jesus and thus one with the Father. Later Jesus will tell them (and us) in John twenty, that just as He was sent into the world, so He is sending them.

You may be struggling with the assertion just made about our being one with Jesus from verse twelve of chapter fourteen. Dear reader I really want you to consider this and ponder it as you continue with this teaching. In chapter seventeen, Jesus demonstrates how very important this concept is. Once again Jesus is truly comparing spiritual to spiritual. The scope of this work does not allow for a full elaboration of this subject; however we will look briefly at one more scripture concerning this Mystery of the Kingdom.

That they all may be one; as thou, Father, art in me, and I in thee, that they also may be one in us: that the world may believe that thou hast sent me. And the glory which thou gavest me I have given them; that they may be one, even as we are one: I in them, and thou in me, that they may be made perfect in one; and that the world may know that thou hast sent me, and hast loved them, as thou hast loved me.
John 17:21-23

Jesus is praying for all of Christianity as He asks two things from Father God. First He asks that we may be with Him and see Him in His full glory that He had with the Father before the foundation of the world. The second is a reference to what He told the twelve in chapter fourteen. In verse 21 He asks Father God to make us one with Him and the Father in just the same way that they are one. Because this request is so important to him, He reiterates it in verse 23. Jesus says that the purpose is so that the world will know that Father God sent Him. WOW! Could this really be true? Did Jesus really mean what He said? What if He did mean it? The idea that we are one with Christ and Father God cannot be taught nor learned; it must be revealed. The early church 'got-it' but in modern times has neglected it, rejected it, and demeaned it. It is now being re-revealed as a Mystery of the Kingdom hidden in plain sight for this generation. For a full discussion of this and much more see *The Law and the Gospel by Fred Gregory*

    Jesus talked to Nicodemus about seeing and entering into the Kingdom of God. Usually we consider that to mean that we get to go to Heaven if we are born again. While that is true, Jesus is really referring to the Kingdom of God on Earth. When he taught the disciples and us by extension, to pray; the first thing that He said to ask for was **"...Thy kingdom come, Thy will be done on earth as in heaven."** Almost all of Jesus' teaching had to do with The Kingdom which He brought with Him in measure and left us in charge of until His return. Jesus taught that He brought The Kingdom of God with Him, so why did he teach us to pray for the Kingdom to Come? This is a MYSTERY HIDDEN FROM CREATION FOR THIS GENERATION. See *Son of God; Son of Man by Fred Gregory*

    There are additional Mysteries that have been hidden for this generation in plain sight from Creation. Our Lord wants to reveal them now. These are pure undiluted spiritual revelations. Many of them will be controversial in-your-face concepts that will be rejected by a lot of religious traditionalists.

    Much, but not all of the 'raw' spiritual revelation that *YOU* will receive from Holy Spirit will be concerning *MYSTERIES OF THE KINGDOM.*

CHAPTER 7

SOZO/SHABAR

Very good examples of a Mysteries of the Kingdom revealed to this generation are two sister ministries that are headquartered at Bethel Church of Redding California called *BETHEL SOZO* and *SHABAR*. This revolutionary concept called Bethel Sozo was hidden in plain sight until it was revealed to the world in 1997. Then a couple of years later another ministry was birthed from Bethel Church that is akin to SOZO. It is the *SHABAR* Ministry[1]. The following is but my own superficial understanding of these amazing ministries. For more detail visit www.ibethel.com or www.bethelsozo.com

Sozo is the Greek word used in the New Testament that is usually translated into English as Salvation. *That if you confess with your mouth Jesus is Lord and believe in your heart that God raised Him from the dead you shall be saved* ***(Sozo).*** Rom 10:9

For by grace are ye saved ***(Sozo)*** *through faith; and that not of your selves it is a gift of God. Ephesians 2:8*

So far this is not new revelation. Most of The Church has known for generations that Sozo means to be saved or born again. That is the most important part of all. However, if we stop there, we leave much on the table that Jesus provided for us. Holy Spirit chose this word carefully. Although Sozo is most often translated saved or salvation, it carries with it other benefits for us. Let's take a look at the definition from the Strong's Greek Lexicon.[2]

sozo *sode'-zo*

from a primary sos (contraction for obsolete saos, "safe"); to save, i.e. deliver or protect (literally or figuratively):--heal, preserve, save (self), do well, be (make) whole.

In Acts 14:9 we read, *"The same heard Paul speak: who stedfastly beholding him, and perceiving that he had faith to be healed **(Sozo).**"* This is just one example where Sozo is used for healing.

Deliverance from a demon is proclaimed in Luke 8:36. *And those who had seen it reported to them how the man who was demon-possessed had been made well. **(Sozo)***

We can see a pattern emerging from this word Sozo: salvation for the spirit; deliverance for the soul; and healing for the body. Jesus provided for the whole man with his sacrifice. Unfortunately, much of the modern church denies both healing and deliverance, so the mystery of Sozo is still hidden to them. However, a growing remnant of The Church does embrace healing of the body and deliverance from unclean spirits that hinder our walk with the Lord.

All of this is enlightening, but it certainly does not rise to the level of being a Mystery of the Kingdom, hidden in plain sight, for this generation. Sometimes these mysteries are revealed when Holy Spirit connects more than one passage by the Rhema of the Word; so it is with Sozo.

LUKE 4:18

The next passages are but two of the places in the Holy Writ where the Mysteries behind these two amazing ministries are hidden in plain sight. In some respects the Sozo and Shabar Ministries are distinctive and in some areas they overlap.

When Jesus went to the temple in Luke 4:18, he read from the book of Isaiah, *"The Spirit of the Lord is upon me, because he hath anointed me to preach the gospel to the poor; he hath sent me to heal the brokenhearted, to preach deliverance to the captives, and recovering of sight to the blind, to set at liberty them that are bruised; To preach the acceptable year of the Lord."*

And he closed the book, and he gave it again to the minister, and sat down. And the eyes of all them that were in the synagogue were fastened on him. And he began to say unto them, This day is this scripture fulfilled in your ears.

NOTE: If you will notice, Jesus stopped in the middle of a sentence and rolled up the scroll. (See Isaiah 61:1) Why did He stop there? We'll answer that in a bit. For now let's look at the original Greek that Holy Spirit used to gain greater insight as to what His intent is here and what Jesus' intent was when He read it.

Preach euaggelizo to announce good news *("evangelize")* especially the gospel:--declare, bring (declare, show) glad (good) tidings, preach (the gospel).

Poor ptochosa beggar (as cringing), i.e. pauper (strictly denoting absolute or public mendicancy, although also used in a qualified or relative sense; whereas 3993 properly means only straitened circumstances in private), literally (often as noun) or figuratively (distressed):--beggar(-ly), poor.

Heal ee-ah'-om-ahee middle voice of apparently a primary verb; to cure (literally or figuratively):--heal, make whole.

Brokenhearted Suntribo to *crush completely, i.e. to shatter* (literally or figuratively):--break (in pieces), broken to shivers (+ -hearted), bruise.

kardia (Latin cor, "heart"); the heart, i.e. (figuratively) the *thoughts or feelings (mind)*; also (by analogy) the middle:--(+ broken-)heart(-ed).

Preach kay-roos'-so to herald (as a public crier), especially divine truth (the gospel):--preacher(-er), *proclaim*, publish.

Deliverance aphesis freedom; (figuratively) pardon:--deliverance, forgiveness, liberty, remission.

Captives aichmalotos a prisoner of war, i.e. (genitive case) a captive:--captive.

Sight anablepsis restoration of sight:--recovery of sight.

Blind tuphlos opaque (as if smoky), i.e. (by analogy) blind (physically or *mentally):--blind.*

Set apostello set apart, i.e. (by implication) to send out (properly, on a mission) literally or figuratively:--put in, send (away, forth, out), set (at liberty).

Liberty aphesis freedom; (figuratively) pardon:--deliverance, forgiveness, liberty, remission.

Bruised thrauo to crush:--bruise. From **rhegnumi** *hrayg'-noo-mee* both prolonged forms of rheko (which appears only in certain forms, and is itself probably a strengthened form of agnumi (see in 2608)) to "break," "wreck" or "crack", i.e. (especially) to sunder (by *separation of the parts*; 2608 being its intensive (with the preposition in composition), and 2352 *a shattering to minute fragments*; but not a reduction to the constituent particles, like 3089) or disrupt, lacerate; by implication, to convulse (with spasms);

114

figuratively, to give vent to joyful emotions:--break (forth), burst, rend, tear.

Isa 61:1

The Spirit of the Lord GOD is upon me; because the LORD hath anointed me to preach good tidings unto the meek; he hath sent me to bind up the brokenhearted, to proclaim liberty to the captives, and the opening of the prison to them that are bound; To proclaim the acceptable year of the LORD, and the day of vengeance of our God;

We will now take a look at the Hebrew words selected by Holy Spirit to communicate to us through the pen of Isaiah. Remember there were two different writers, Luke and Isaiah who were separated by hundreds of years, but one author—God, The Holy Spirit.

Preach basar *baw-sar'* a primitive root; properly, to be fresh, i.e. full (rosy, (figuratively) cheerful); to announce (glad news):-- messenger, preach, publish, shew forth, (bear, bring, carry, preach, good, tell good) tidings.

Meek `anav *aw-nawv'* or (by intermixture with 6041) Aanayv {aw-nawv'}; from 6031; ***depressed (figuratively), in mind*** (gentle) or circumstances (needy, especially saintly):--humble, lowly, meek, poor.

Bind up chabash *khaw-bash'* a primitive root; to wrap firmly (especially a turban, compress, or saddle); figuratively, to stop, to rule:--bind (up), ***gird*** about, govern, healer, put, saddle, wrap about.

Broken-hearted leb shabar labe *shaw-bar'*

a primitive root; to burst (literally or figuratively):--***break (down, off, in pieces***, up), broken((-hearted)), bring to the birth, crush, destroy, hurt, quench, X quite, tear, view (by mistake for 7663).

Proclaim qara' *kaw-raw'*
a primitive root (rather identical with 7122 through the idea of accosting a person met); ***to call out*** to (i.e. properly, address by name, but used in a wide variety of applications):--bewray (self), that are bidden, call (for, forth, self, upon), cry (unto), (be) famous, guest, invite, mention, (give) name, preach, (make) proclaim(-ation), pronounce, publish, read, renowned, say.

Liberty d@rowr *der-ore'*
from an unused root (meaning to move rapidly); ***freedom***; hence, spontaneity of outflow, and so clear:--liberty, pure.

Captives shabah *shaw-baw'*
a primitive root; ***to transport into captivity***:--(bring away, carry, carry away, lead, lead away, take) captive(-s), drive (take) away.

Opening of Prision p@qach-qowach *pek-akh-ko'-akh*
from 6491 redoubled; opening (of a dungeon), i.e. jail-delivery (figuratively, salvation for sin):--opening of the prison.

Bound 'acar *aw-sar'*
a primitive root; to yoke or hitch; by analogy, to fasten in any sense, to join battle:--bind, fast, gird, harness, hold, keep, make ready, order, prepare, prison(-er), put in bonds, set in array, tie.

SUMMERY OF ISAIAH 61 AND LUKE 4

I don't know if I could live with myself, as a teacher of the Word of God, if I didn't pause a moment from advancing the primary focus of this work to piqué your interest in these two scriptures. They, taken together are a gold mine of insight that can be used in correlating Old and New Testament theology and prophesy. What Isaiah writes is presented almost verbatim in Luke. We can prayerfully compare each word for a deeper understanding of the messages. One of those gold nuggets is the answer to the question raised earlier. Why did Jesus not finish the sentence?

Well, why didn't He? That day in the temple He began to fulfill all that He had just read of the prophecy in Isaiah; however this last part has yet to be fulfilled. This is a good lesson for studying scripture. The fulfillment of the two parts has already been separated by more than 2,000 years. The day of vengeance of our God is yet future. Many other prophecies do not make sense until one realizes that there is more than one event described within one sentence or paragraph.

Now back to our focus. While it is obvious that Luke 4:18 and following is not the full range of Jesus ministry and purpose on the Earth, it is however, vitally important and for the most part, we in the Church have missed it for far too long. By comparing the Hebrew with the Greek we can get a fuller understanding and get a better grasp of what the Sozo Ministry is all about. This by necessity will be a bit tedious. However, if I am correct about this being a Mystery of The Kingdom, hidden in plain sight from the powers of this world and for our glory; it is just too important not to address.

Remember that after He had read the scripture from Isaiah, Jesus made a bold statement that could have gotten Him stoned and kicked out of the Temple. All who were with Him knew exactly what He was inferring. He was saying, "I am the long awaited Messiah." What parts of His vast ministry began that day? Let's see.

The first part of the Ministry that Jesus claimed for Himself was to *PREACH* good tidings/the gospel to the poor/meek. So then He was anointed to proclaim, announce, and declare good tidings— to evangelize. Because the word for good news is transliterated from the Greek as Gospel we often assume that it always is the equivalent of the modern day Preacher. This is not always the case. We must look at the context in which it is used and for whom the announcement is intended. The word Gospel may mean all or a part of Jesus' work on the Cross. It may be the Gospel of the Cross or the Gospel of the Kingdom. In this passage, Jesus says that the good news is for the POOR. In Isaiah it is the word MEEK. Is there a difference and if so what is the overlap? The word for poor usually means a beggar or pauper; however, the word in Hebrew for meek also means *depressed in mind.* Could this have been what Jesus meant in the Sermon on the Mount in Matthew 5:3 when He said, "Blessed are the *poor in Spirit*; for theirs is the Kingdom of God." Good News to a beggar or pauper could mean a few more dollars in his jeans, but Good News to the "poor in spirit—the meek," would mean *inner healing.* WOW!

The second aspect of the anointing that Jesus mentioned was 'to heal the brokenhearted.' Isaiah says, "...to bind up the brokenhearted." You will notice above that the word for heal means just that to heal; to cure, to make whole. However, the Hebrew word translated bind up gives us additional revelation. It is often used to tightly wind a turban, tighten a saddle. That is to wrap securely so as to hold together and control something that may be able to come apart. Once we look at the two words translated "brokenhearted," the idea of binding up will be even clearer. The Greek words mean to break the heart/mind/***soul*** into pieces, to crush completely or to shatter. The Hebrew words mean to break into pieces, to crush the ***soul; to separate into parts.*** I think that you now understand the use of the term binding up the brokenhearted. The Hebrew words for brokenhearted are *"shabar lebe."* Bethel Church of Redding Californian's second inner healing ministry founded and led by Teresa Liebscher is called *SHABAR.* In the Shabar ministry, these brokenhearted people are referred to as "Shattered." Other ministries refer to these people as having "fragmented souls."[3]

My, oh my, what a savior we have, but he isn't finished yet. Thirdly, He says that He has been sent to Preach/proclaim/announce deliverance to the captives. Isaiah says. "Proclaim liberty to the captives." We looked at preach or proclaim earlier, so let's now focus our attention on the words deliverance and liberty. Both the Hebrew and Greek word means freedom or deliverance. Remember Sozo also means deliverance. In both scriptures the benefactors of this deliverance are captives. The Hebrew word translated captives is the word for prisoner of war and the Greek word means to transport into captivity. Both words convey the idea that the person has been captured, bound and is being taken to a more permanent place of imprisonment. In the spiritual realm, it indicates one who is being led into captivity by the lies of the enemy. These lies may have their origin in early childhood from a dysfunctional family setting where unhealthy relationships with a Father, Mother, or sibling may have caused them to believe something untrue about Father God, Holy Spirit, or Jesus. Many people are born again and on their way to Heaven, but are still held captive in their mind because they do not know that freedom was part of the package deal that Jesus paid for on the cross. We become a little like elephants. Baby elephants are tethered by strong chains and iron clamps around one leg to large stakes driven into the ground. As a baby, they are not strong enough to pull away. As they grow into full grown bull elephants with tremendous power, they are still tethered with the same stake and chain. One jerk from that massive leg could easily snap the chain or uproot the stake, but the elephant does not know this. Now, his captivity is not real but perceived, but that makes little difference to him. So it is with many believers in Christ. They are held captive by lies and deceit, not aware of the power and authority that they have as a Child of God just to pull away.

The forth area for which Jesus said that He was anointed to accomplish is not recorded in our English translation of Isaiah. He said, "and recovering of sight to the blind." This is the second part of the proclamation. The first part was to preach or proclaim deliverance to the captives and the second part is to preach or proclaim recovering of sight to the blind. If you are like me, you probably thought that that was referring to physical blindness. Stay with me for a tad. This is one of those Mysteries Hidden in Plain Sight. The Greek word rendered recovery of sight usually does refer to physical sight; however, the word for blind can also mean *"mentally blind."* Now, with that understanding that statement doesn't stand out from the other statements as if it were out of place, but flows with the theme. Jesus is saying that He came to proclaim freedom or deliverance to those taken captive by the lies of the enemy and recovering of sight to those who are mentally blinded by those lies.

The Fifth phase of the anointing is the last that we will deal with here. It is worded differently in Luke than it is in Isaiah. Jesus read, "...set at liberty them that are bruised." Isaiah says, "The opening of prison to them that are bound." The word translated bruised in Greek means to break into separate parts, or to shatter into minute fragments. This is quite similar to the Hebrew shabar that is rendered brokenhearted. The opening of prison refers to those who were led captive and have now been thrown into that prison. Not only did Jesus come to free those caught, but to rescue those who have been incarcerated.

Have you noticed that all five of these areas mentioned by Jesus that day in the temple have to do with inner healing of the soul? We have not dealt with these problems very well in the Body of Christ. When we witness people manifesting these things we often judge them as never having "really" been saved or maybe were saved but have "backslid." Either judgment is horrible and just wrong. As noted earlier Paul, under the influence of Holy Spirit in Romans chapter twelve admonishes us to be transformed by the renewing of our mind so that we will prove or manifest the perfect will of God.

The Church has abdicated its responsibility to continue Jesus work with His anointing in ministering to these hurting members of the Body of Christ. What a pity that we have left it to the secular, unbelieving world to do what we refuse to do. In the secular world many of these folks who are prisoners, captives, blind, or brokenhearted have been referred to as being bi-polar, having Multiple Personality Disorder, Dissociate Personality Disorder, or a multitude of other disorders or syndromes. Psychologists and psychiatrists are doing the best they can without the power of Holy Spirit, but we can do better with His power.

Thank God, in the past several years there have been inner healing ministries that have been launched. The ones that I am familiar with are the SOZO Ministry and the SHABAR Ministry of

Bethel Church in Redding California. I am moved to reiterate that I am convinced that these, together represent one of those Mysteries of the Kingdom hidden in plain sight for this generation.

HISTORY OF SOZO BETHEL

Many ministries the Father God ordains in His Church are a combination of other existing ministries that are in no way connected until someone receives a revelation. Then the pieces are put together and the result is greater than the sum of the parts. So it was with Bethel Sozo. Pablo Batari, of Argentina who was Carlos Anacondia's deliverance pastor developed a tool for helping to set new converts free. This tool was called the "Ten Steps." In 1997 a healing evangelist was scheduled to minister at Bethel Church. He sent an advance prayer team ahead to train the local intercessors for the coming event. Pablo's "Ten Steps" was part of that training.

Dawna DeSilva was one of the Bethel prayer team members that received that training and subsequently ministered with these newly acquired tools. The level of freedom for the people ministered to was miraculous. This did not go unnoticed by the pastors of Bethel. Dawna was given the responsibility of leadership in the new ministry with the full covering of the Church.

The "Ten Steps" was condensed to "The Four Doors." Other tools were added such as "The Father Ladder," "The Wall," and "Presenting Jesus." Within a year many other churches ask for the Sozo team to help them start a Sozo ministry. Within ten years Bethel Sozo Ministry had gone all over the world with the International Bethel Sozo Organization[4].

On a personal note; about thirty years ago I begin to get these nudges from Holy Spirit in the form of questions. Some of the questions were: "We have physical healing, why do we not have healing of the emotions or of mental disorders?" "Surely, God these areas aren't too tough for you, are they?" Of course the resounding answer was, "No!" I thank you Father for revealing these Mysteries of the Kingdom to this generation.

In the late spring of 2012 my prayers and questions were answered. I heard about Bethel Sozo and attended an introductory seminar at my home church near Birmingham Alabama. Since then, I have had the great honor of being a member of Sozo Birmingham led by Brannon Nix, who received his degree in Prophetic Ministry from Bethel. I have the privilege of continuing the ministry of Jesus that He started that day in the temple. Each week, I get to be the facilitator and watch as Father, Son, and Holy Spirit open the eyes of those who are mentally blind, set the captives free, open prison doors for those who are incarcerated, and bind up the brokenhearted.

Just *imagine* what new ministry for this generation Father God will birth through *you* just as he did Dawna DeSilva and Teresa Liebscher. Are you tingling with anticipation? The excitement is almost too much to bear.

CHAPTER 8

THE SECRET PLACE OF THE MOST HIGH

Okay, each of you must now enter the airlock and seal the door behind you. (I am entering my airlock, also.) This is the place where you and I will begin to receive pure Mystery Revealing Revelations. All of the air will be sucked out of the airlock; that is all of the cares of this world; all of those issues that are on your plate. When you are ready, *YOU* will have to activate the switch that opens the outer door yourself. When it is opened, you will be exposed to the void of space with your Faithsuit as your only protection. Then you will make the decision to leap toward your spiritual destiny.

I have taken you as far as my anointing as a teacher will allow me to go. You are now in the airlock. This airlock is called *"The Secret Place of The Most High."*

He that *dwells in the secret place of the most High shall abide under the shadow of the Almighty.* Psalms 91:1

And I will give thee the treasures of darkness, and hidden riches of secret places, that thou may know that I, the LORD, which call thee by thy name, am the God of Israel. Isa. 45:3

Dear reader, you and I and others like us can relate to the characters in the movie "Close Encounters of the Third Kind." They were obsessed with something they didn't understand. They were *invited* to a landmark called of all things "The Devil's Toothpick." One lady drew dozens of pictures of it and the main character built it in his living room and lost his family in his pursuit. Of course that movie was all make believe, but we who have been invited by our Lord to come to the *secret place of the most high* can relate to that passion and drive as well as that frustration.

I truly believe that *access* is by invitation only, it is not by performance but by grace. *The fire in your belly that refuses to be extinguished, the gnawing that cannot be satisfied, the eternal craving for intimacy with Jesus, is your invitation to the secret place of the Most High.*

Just as it was in the first century when those mysteries were revealed, it was the duty of the ones who received the revelations to act upon them and to tell others. *Are you ready?*

There are two things that you might consider before making that leap:

1. Put one more call in to God on his private line **Jer.** 33:3
2. Pray our prayer again

That the God of our Lord Jesus Christ, the Father of glory, may give unto you the spirit of SOPHISTICATED WISDOM AND DISCLOSURE in the FULL DISCERNMENT OF HIM.

And that the VISION of your IMAGINATION being ENGULFED IN HIS LIGHT that you may know

What is the hope of his calling [invitation]
What are the riches of the glory of his inheritance in the saints
What is the exceeding great power to us who believe
YOUR CHALLENGE—YOUR INVITATION

I don't know how long you will be in the Airlock called The Secret Place of the Most High and I do not know how many times you will return to it. Many I hope. For a number of you this will be the very first time that you realized that this intimacy with Father God was even possible. As you enter again and again into the Secret Place of the Most High, bear in mind the declaration of Psalms 91:1 *He that DWELLS in that secret place of the most high will ABIDE under the shadow of the Almighty.* Not only can you enter that place time and time again, but Father God's goal is for you and me to live there; to walk in that intimacy with Him constantly. I submit this to you; the more frequently that we "visit' that place, the more at home we will feel. My personal soaking time with the Lord is in the morning after the grandkids have gone to school. I like to ask Father God to sit on His lap. He always allows me to do just that. I will myself to lay aside all of my problems and requests and just "be with my Papa." From His lap, I eventually ask Him to take me to *The Secret Place of the Most High.* That is one of the times that He chooses to download revelation to me. I am becoming so addicted to that experience. I know that you will, too. *Whee!* Let's catch our breath for a minute after that.

As you completely release all that you are to the Lord in that place of intimacy, *you may come to realize that just since you began reading the pages of this manuscript you have already begun to receive 'raw' undiluted Mystery Revelation from Holy Spirit that was hidden in plain sight.*

Maybe, the swirling in your mind (imagination) has begun to slow down a bit. Perhaps the gnawing is finding some outlet. Hopefully, the burning in your belly is starting to find focus.

Holy Spirit often reveals nugget concepts to our spirit that we did not know and they are meant for our enlightenment as we expose ourselves to Jesus. *However be aware that in this hour that that nugget may never have been revealed to the Body of Christ before. WOW!*

****

YOUR FIRST HIDDEN MYSTERY REVEALED

While you are still soaring with Holy Spirit from appropriating that prophesy for yourself; while you are still basking in the manifest presence of The Lord; before you come down I want to toss you one last *DIAMOND*.

Your first hidden mystery is in the prayer itself; the one that we have been praying all along this journey. I am just confirming what Holy Spirit has already shown you.

May the VISION of your IMAGINATION be truly ENGULFED IN HIS LIGHT.

That verse is without a natural illustration. There is no parable or analogy to explain it. It is pure. Embrace it. It is your entrance to the Revelation of Mysteries for this generation; your gateway to *Treasures of Darkness.*

Please Stop reading and spend whatever time you need in the airlock of the secret place of the Most High alone with Jesus before proceeding.

Now that the Lord has satisfied the need in your spirit for a while; by the faith *of God* you have fuller discernment of Jesus; and have your imagination more fully engulfed in the light of your true identity in Jesus, it is time to open the outer airlock door and

LEAP...

ENDNOTES

IMAGINATION

Chapter 1

1. Wheaties a product of General Mills *Wheaties, Breakfast o Champions* slogan first introduced in 1927
2. THE DESCENT OF MAN, 1871 Charles Darwin
3. Anthony Sinclair, "The Art of the Ancients," *Nature* 426 (2003): 774-75.
4. Ian Tattersall and Jeffrey Schwartz, "Evolution of the Genus Homo," *Annual Review of Earth and Planetary Sciences* 37 (May 2009): 81
5. Christopher S. Henshilwood et al., "Emergence of Modern Human Behavior: Middle Stone Age Engravings from South Africa," *Science* 295 (February 15, 2002): 1278–80; — Henshilwood et al., "Middle Stone Age Shell Beads from South Africa," *Science* 304 (April 16, 2004): 404; Lyn Wadley et al., "Implications for Complex Cognition from the Hafting of Tools with Compound Adhesives in the Middle Stone Age, South Africa," *Proceedings of the National Academy of Sciences*, USA 106 (2009): 9590–94; Kyle S. Brown et al., "Fire as an Engineering Tool of Early Modern Humans," *Science* 325 (August 14, 2009): 859–62; Vincent Mourre et al., "Early Use of Pressure Flaking on Lithic Artifacts at Blombos Cave, South Africa," *Science* 330 (October 26, 2010): 659–62; Pierre-Jean Texier et al., "A Howiesons Poort Tradition of Engraving Ostrich Eggshell Containers Dated to 60,000 Years Ago at Diepkloof Rock Shelter, South Africa," *Proceedings of the National Academy of Sciences*, USA 107 (April 6, 2010): 6180–85; Lyn Wadley et al., "Middle Stone Age Bedding Construction and

Settlement Patterns at Sibudu, South Africa," *Science* 334 (December 9, 2011): 1388–91.
6. THINK AND GROW RICH! By Napoleon Hill 2004 version published by Ross Cornwell (ISBN 1-59330-200-2)

Chapter 2

1. TIME TO DEFEAT THE EVIL Chuck D. Pierce Copyright 2011 Chuck D. Pierce
2. All rights reserved Publisher: Charisma House Charisma Media/Charisma House Book Group 600 Rinehart Road Lake Mary, Fl 32746
3. Kathie Walter Ministries www.kathiewalter.com
4. Christopher Blackeby of Field of Dreams Church, Adelaide, Australia www.chrisblackeby.com

Chapter 4

1. "The Supernatural Power of a Transformed Mind" Bill Johnson Bethel Church Redding, Cal CD teaching series www.ibethel.org
2. "I will arise and Go now" (Lines 37-40) Ogden Nash

Chapter 5

1. THE NAVAJO CODE TALKERS by Major Howard M. Conner(Aaseng, *Navajo Code Talkers*, page 32
2. THE NAVAJO CODE TALKERS by Major Howard M. Conner(Aaseng, *Navajo Code Talkers*, page 32
3. THE NAVAJO CODE TALKERS by Major Howard M. Conner(Aaseng, *Navajo Code Talkers*, page 32

Chapter 6

1. "The Supernatural Power of a Transformed Mind" Bill Johnson Bethel Church Redding, Cal CD teaching series www.ibethel.org

Chapter 7

1. SOZO BASIC MANUAL Copyright 2011—Sozo Ministry Bethel Church 915 Twin View Blvd Redding Cal 96003 (page 10)
2. STRONG'S Greek and Hebrew Dictionaries
3. ADVANCED SOZO DVD SET Bethel Church 915 Twin View Blvd Redding, Cal 96003
4. SOZO BASIC MANUAL Copyright 2011—Sozo Ministry Bethel Church 915 Twin View Blvd Redding Cal 96003 (page 10,28,29,39,and45)

OTHER MYSTERIES OF THE KINGDOM VOLUMES BY THE AUTHOR

WHO IS MAN

WILL THE REAL LUCIFER PLEASE STAND UP?

SON OF GOD/ SON OF MAN

I AM: THE SOVEREIGNTY OF GOD

THE LAW AND THE GOSPEL

BEYOND THE GIFTS OF THE SPIRIT

RIGHT MIND

GIFTS OF THE FATHER, SON, AND HOLY SPIRIT

Made in the USA
Charleston, SC
06 October 2014